BABY NAMES FOR GIRLS

JAMES DALBY

FORWARD

Choosing a name for your baby is probably one of the most important decisions you can make in your child's life. It can affect her attitudes towards herself and others and how she perceives herself in relation to the rest of society. Choosing the wrong name for your child can leave her feeling like she doesn't belong or fit in.

Take into consideration what you would feel like if you grew up as Chester and was constantly called the common nickname 'Chester the molester.' There are a great number of names that lend themselves to taunting and teasing, simply because of the immaturity of other people. This can affect a child's self-esteem, or even leave her prone to being bullied for no reason.

Consider your ancestry. If you are of English descent, consider names of Queens like Elizabeth or Mary. If you are of Russian decent, consider Czars like Catherine. Naming your baby based on your cultural heritage is a common method, and usually turns out pretty well.

Another interesting trend is to name your child based on a location. You can call your little girl Florida, Atlanta, or Alberta. This trend is fairly recent, as is more common in boys.

Have some common sense. Would you want to grow up with the name you are considering for your child? That should pretty much sum up the decision making process when you are choosing your baby's name.

It's your decision, but be open to other people's ideas. Sometimes a suggestion of a friend or family member hits the nail on the head. Also, be certain to take your spouse's opinion into consideration, because it's their child too. In fact, it is common to name a child after a family member such as your parent or grandparent.

In this list of 5000+ girls baby names, duplicates are kept to a minimum so that more names could be included in the list. This is by no means a complete list, but is has a wide variety of names from different origins, and have a diverse set of meanings. You'll be sure to come up with some good ideas from these suggestions.

NAME	**ORIGIN**	**MEANING**
Aaliyah	Arabic, Hebrew	High exalted, to ascend.
Aasia	Hindu	
Aba	African	Born on Thursday
Abbey	Hebrew	Father's joy. From Abigail.
Abbie	Hebrew	Father's joy. From Abigail.
Abby	Hebrew	Father's joy. From Abigail.
Abelia	Hebrew	Breath. The feminine form of Abel.
Abella	Assyrian	Child.
Abeo	Nigerian	Happy she was born.
Abey	Native American	Leaf.
Abha	Hindu	Lustrous beauty, shining.
Abhilasha	Hindu	
Abia	Arabic	Great.
Abigail	Hebrew	Father's joy.
Abijah	Hebrew	The Lord is my father.
Abilene		The name of a city in Texas.
Abina	Ghanian	Born on a Thursday.
Abiona	Yoruban	Born on a journey.
Abir	Arabic/Hebrew	Arabic: The fragrant one. Hebrew: Strong.
Abira	Hebrew	Strong.
Abra	Hebrew	The father of many. The feminine form of Abraham.
Abrianna		Mother of many nations.
Abrienda	Spanish	Opening.
Acacia	Greek	Thorny, as in the Acacia tree.

Acadia	Canadian	
Acanit	Ugandan	Difficult times.
Acantha	Greek	A legendary nymph.
Accalia	Latin	The foster mother of Romulus and Remus, the founders of Rome.
Acedia	Czech	
Achal	Hindu	Steady, mountainous.
Achazia	Hebrew	The Lord holds.
Achen	Ugandan	A twin.
Achilla	Greek	A handsome figure in Greek mythology. The feminine form of Achilles.
Achit	Hindu	
Achlys	Greek	Mist, darkness.
Ada	Teutonic	Prosperous and joyful, happy.
Adabelle		Joyous and beautiful. From Ada and Belle.
Adah	Hebrew	Adornment or ornament. A biblical name.
Adalgisa	Old German	Noble hostage.
Adalia	Hebrew	God is my refuge.
Adama	Hebrew	Of the red earth. The feminine form of Adam.
Adamina		The Earth.
Adamma		Beautiful child.
Adana		A city in Turkey.
Adar	Hebrew	Fire.
Adara	Greek/Arabic	Greek: Beauty. Arabic: Virgin.
Addi	French	Noble and kind.
Addie	French	Noble and kind.
Addisyn	French	Noble and kind.
Addy	French	Noble and kind.
Adela	French	Noble and serene.
Adelaide	Old German	Noble and kind.
Adele	French	Noble and kind.
Adelicia	Old English	Noble and kind. Form of Adelaide and Alice.
Adelina	Old German	Noble.
Adelinda	French	Noble and kind.
Adeline	French	Noble, kind.
Adelle	French	Noble, kind.

Adelpha	Greek	Sisterly.
Ademia	Greek	Without husband.
Aden	Arabic	Fiery one.
Adena	Hebrew	Delicate, sensual.
Adeola	Nigerian	A crown.
Aderes	Hebrew	One who protects.
Aderyn	Welsh	A bird.
Adesina	Yoruban	The way is opened for more.
Adhira	Hindu	Lightning.
Adiba	Arabic	Cultured.
Adie	Hebrew	Ornament.
Adiel	Hebrew	An ornament of God.
Adila	Arabic	Equal, like.
Adima	Teutonic	Noble, famous.
Adina	Hebrew	Slender and delicate. A biblical name.
Adishree	Hindu	Exalted.
Aditi	Hindu	Free and unbounded.
Adiva	Arabic	Pleasant, gentle.
Adolfina	German	Noble wolf, noble hero.
Adolpha	Teutonic	A noble she-wolf. The feminine version of Adolf.
Adona	Spanish	Sweet.
Adoncia	Spanish	Sweet.
Adonia	Greek	A beautiful goddess. The feminine form of Adonis.
Adora	Latin	The adored one.
Adorabelle		A combination of Adora and Belle.
Adorna	Latin	Adorned with jewels.
Adriana	Latin	A dark woman from the sea. The feminine form of Adrian. Generally an Italian name.
Adriano	Greek	Dark, rich.
Adrienne		Dark, rich.
Aegea	Greek	Of the Aegean.
Aemilia		From Shakespeare's play Comedy of Errors
Aeryn		
Affrica	Celtic	Pleasant. Also from the name of the continent.
Afina	Rumanian	Blueberry.

Afra	African	Dust.
Afraima	Arabic/Hebrew	Fruitful.
Afric	Celtic	Pleasant.
Africa	Celtic	Pleasant.
Afton	Old English	River name.
Agape	Greek	Love.
Agate	French	A precious stone.
Agatha	Greek	Good, kind, honorable. St. Agatha was a 3rd-century Sicilian martyr.
Aggie		Good.
Aglaia	Greek	Splendor, splendid beauty. The goddess of harmony.
Agnes	Greek	Pure, chaste. The name of a saint of the Middle Ages.
Agneta	Greek, Germanic	Pure.
Ahava	Hebrew	Name of a river, love.
Ahimsa	Hindu	Nonviolent virtue.
Ahnada		A city in Portugal.
Ahneta	Latin	Ambitious.
Ahuva	Hebrew	Beloved.
Ai	Japanese	Love.
Aida		Helper.
Aidan	Irish Gaelic	The little fiery one.
Aide		Prosperous and joyful, happy.
Aideen		Shining, bright.
Aiesha	Arabic	Woman.
Aijah		
Aiko	Japanese	The little loved one, the beloved.
Aila	Finnish	Light-bearer.
Aileen	Scottish	The light of the sun. The Irish form of Helen.
Ailis	Irish Gaelic	The light of the sun. Form of Alice.
Ailish	Irish Gaelic	A form of Elizabeth, meaning consecrated to God.
Ailsa	Scottish	After a rocky inlet known as Ailsa Craig.
Aimee	French	Beloved. A form of Amy.
Ain	Arabic	Precious, eye.
Aina	Yoruban	Complicated delivery.

Aine	Irish Gaelic	Brightness, radiance. Traditional name of the queen of the fairies in Celtic mythology.
Aingeal	Irish Gaelic	A heavenly messenger, an angel. Form of Angela.
Ainhoa	Basque	Reverence to Virgin Mary.
Ainsley	Old English/Scottish	A meadow or clearing. Also a unisex name.
Aintzane	Basque	Glorious.
Airlia	Greek	Ethereal.
Aisha	Arabic	Life. The name of Mohamed's third and favorite wife.
Aisling		A vision or dream.
Aislinn		A vision or dream.
Aissa	African	Grateful.
Aithne	Celtic	Little fire.
Aiyana	Native American	Eternal bloom.
Aja		
Ajay	Hindu	Unconquerable, God.
Akaisha	Irish	The akaisha flower.
Akako	Japanese	Red.
Akala	Aboriginal	A parrot.
Akana		A mountain in Papua, New Guinea.
Akanke	Nigerian	To know her is to love her.
Akanksha	Hindu	
Akasma	Turkish	White climbing rose.
Akela	Hawaiian	Noble.
Akila	Arabic	Wise.
Akilah	Arabic	Intelligent, logical.
Akili	Tanzanian	Wisdom.
Akilina	Latin	Eagle.
Akina	Japanese	A Spring flower.
Akriti	Hindu	
Aksana	Russian	
Akshita	Hindu	
Akuti	Hindu	Princess.
Alaine		The bright fair one, the beautiful child.
Alake	Yoruban	One petted.
Alala	Greek	Goddess of war.
Alameda	Spanish	A Poplar tree.

Alana	Irish Gaelic	The bright fair one, the beautiful child.
Alani	Hawaiian	An orange tree.
Alankrita	Hindu	
Alanna		The bright fair one, the beautiful child.
Alaqua	Native American	A sweet gum tree.
Alarice	Teutonic	The ruler of all. The feminine form of Alaric.
Alastrina	Greek	The protector of mankind. The feminine form of Alastair.
Alatea	Spanish from Greek	Truth.
Alavda	French	Lark.
Alazne	Basque	Miracle.
Alba	Aboriginal	A sand hill. Also see Albina.
Alberta	Teutonic	Noble and illustrious. The feminine form of Albert, and also the name of a Canadian province.
Albina	Latin	A white lady, someone of very fair hair and color
Albinka	Latin	Blond.
Alcina	Greek	Strong-minded. A sorceress in Greek mythology.
Alda	Teutonic	Wise and rich.
Aldabella	Italian	Beautiful. From Leda and Bell.
Aldara	Greek	A winged gift.
Aldea	Teutonic	Rich.
Aldercy	Old English	A chief.
Aldonza	Spanish	Sweet.
Aldora	Old English	Of noble rank.
Alejandra	Spanish	The defender, or helper of mankind. Feminine form of Alexander.
Aleka	Greek	The defender, or helper of mankind. Form of Alexandra.
Aleksandra		The defender, or helper of mankind. Form of Alexandra.
Aleksia	Danish/Norwegian	The defender, or helper of mankind. Form of Alexandra.
Alena		A woman from the village of Magdala.
Aleshanee	Native American	She plays all the time
Alessa		Protector of mankind.

Alessandra	Italian	The defender, or helper of mankind. Form of Alexandra.
Alesti		
Aleta		The little winged one.
Alethea	Greek	Truthful.
Alex		The defender, or helper of mankind. A form of Alexander.
Alexa		Protector of mankind.
Alexandra	Greek	The defender, or helper of mankind.
Alexandria		Defender of mankind.
Alexavia		A form of Alex.
Alexia		The defender, or helper of mankind.
Alexina		The defender, or helper of mankind.
Alexis	Greek	The protector and helper of mankind.
Alfonsa	Teutonic	Noble and ready. Feminine form of Alphonse.
Alfreda	Teutonic	A wise counselor. Feminine form of Alfred.
Algerine		Woman from Algeria.
Ali	Arabic	Exalted, or noble.
Alia		Noble, descender.
Alice	Greek/Teutonic	Greek: The wise counsellor, or the truthful one. Teutonic: Noble. The name became popular after the publication of Lewis Carroll's Alice in Wonderland books. Also see Alicia and Alison.
Alicia	Greek/Teutonic	Greek: The wise counselor, or the truthful one. Teutonic: Noble. A form of Alice, but often used as an independent name.
Alida	Latin	The little winged one.
Alike	Nigerian	girl who drives out beautiful women
Alima	Arabic	Skilled in dancing and music.
Alina		Noble and kind. Also see Adele.
Aline		Noble and kind. Also see Adele.
Alinga	Aboriginal	The sun.
Alisa	Italian	The wise counselor, or the truthful one. Also see Alicia and Alison.

Alisha	Greek/Teutonic	Greek The wise counselor, or the truthful one. Teutonic Noble. Also see Alicia and Alison.
Alison	Old English	The light of the sun.
Alissa	Greek	Truth, noble.
Alita	Spanish	noble
Alithia	Greek/Teutonic	Greek The wise counselor, or the truthful one. Teutonic Noble. Also see Alicia and Alison.
Aliya	Arabic/Hebrew	Arabic: Sublime, exalted. Hebrew: To ascend.
Aliz	Hungarian	Kind.
Aliza	Modern Jewish	Joy.
Alize		One who charms.
Alka	Polish	Noble, brilliant.
Alkina	Aboriginal	The moon.
Alkira	Aboriginal	The sky.
Allayna		
Allegra	Italian/Spanish	Cheerful, joyous.
Allene		Attractive, peaceful.
Allie		The defender, or helper of mankind. From the name Alexandra, Alice or Alison.
Allirea	Aboriginal	Quartz.
Allison		Of noble birth.
Allora	Aboriginal	The place of the swamp. The name of a town in Queensland.
Allunga	Aboriginal	The sun.
Allyson		Of noble birth.
Alma	Latin/Celtic	Latin: Of the soul. Celtic: Good.
Almeda		Ambitious.
Almedha	Welsh	Shapely.
Almira	Arabic	Truth without question.
Alodia		The light of the sun. Form of Alice.
Alodie	Old English	Wealthy, prosperous.
Aloha	Hawaiian	Greetings.
Alohi	Hawaiian	Brilliant.
Alona	Hebrew	From the Oak tree.
Alonsa		Noble and ready. Feminine form of Alphonse.
Alonza		Noble and ready. Feminine form of Alphonse.

Alouetta		The little winged one.
Aloysia		A famous warrior maiden. The feminine form of Louis.
Alpa	Hindu	
Alpha	Greek	The first one. First letter of the Greek alphabet. Used in biblical references.
Alta	Latin	Tall.
Altair	Arabic, Greek	Bird, star.
Althea	Greek	The healer, or wholesome.
Altheda	Greek	Flower-like.
Alula	Latin	A star in Ursa Major.
Aluma	Hebrew	A girl.
Alumit	Hebrew	Secret.
Alva	Latin	The white or blonde one. Also a nickname from Alvina.
Alvina	Teutonic	A beloved and noble friend. The feminine form of Alvin. Also see Elvina.
Alvira	Latin/Teutonic	Latin: The fair one. Teutonic: A true stranger.
Alvita	Latin	Vivacious, full of life.
Alyna		Noble and kind. Also see Adele.
Alysa	Greek	princess
Alysia	Greek	Possessive. Also see Alicia.
Alyson		Of noble birth.
Alyssa	Greek	The sane one. Also a form of Alicia.
Alzena	Arabic	A woman.
Ama	Ghanian	Born on Saturday.
Amabel	Latin	Lovable, the sweet one. Also see Mabel.
Amadea	Latin	Beloved of God.
Amadi	Nigerian	General rejoicing, seemed destined to die at.
Amadika	Zimbabwean	The beloved one.
Amadis	Latin	Love of God.
Amadora	Italian	The gift of love.
Amaia	Basque	End.
Amala	Arabic	Hope. Also see Amelia.
Amalie	Teutonic	Industrious, striving. Also see Emily.
Amana	Hebrew	Faithful or loyal.

Amanda	Latin	Worthy of being loved.
Amandeep	Hindu	Light of peace.
Amandine	Latin	Beloved.
Amandla	African	Power.
Amani	Arabic	An aspiration, a desire.
Amara	Greek	Unfading or eternal beauty.
Amarante	French	Flower name.
Amaranth	Greek	An unfading flower.
Amarina	Aboriginal	Rain.
Amaris	Hebrew	God has promised.
Amaryllis	Greek	A shepherdess. Also a flower name.
Amata	Italian/Spanish	Beloved. Form of Amy.
Amaya		
Amazonia	Greek	Warlike. Also after the Amazon River.
Ambar	Sanskrit	Of the sky.
Amber	Arabic	A gemstone.
Amberjill	Old English	
Amberley	Hindu	The sky.
Ambika	Hindi	A mother.
Ambra	Arabic	After the gemstone amber.
Ambria		
Ambrosine	Greek	The divine immortal one. The feminine form of Ambrose.
Amdis	Latin	Immortal.
Ameerah	Arabic	Princess.
Amelia	Teutonic	Industrious, striving. Also see Emily.
Amelinda		Industrious, striving. Formed from Amelia and Linda.
Amena		Honest woman.
Ames	Latin	Loves.
Amethyst	Greek	The name of a semi-precious stone.
Ami	Japanese	Friend.
Amice	Latin	Friendship.
Amina	Arabic	Honest, faithful.
Aminta	Greek	The protector.
Amira	Arabic/Hebrew	Arabic: A princess. Hebrew: Speech.
Amisha	Hindu	

Amissa	Hebrew	Friend.
Amita	Hindu	Without limits.
Amitola	Native American	Rainbow.
Amity	Latin	Friendship. Also see Amice.
Amoke	Yoruban	To pet her.
Amorina		Love.
Amorita	Latin	The little beloved one.
Amrita	Sanskrit	Immortal.
Amy	Old French	Beloved. Also a nickname from Amelia.
An	Chinese/Vietnamese	Chinese: Peace. Vietnamese: Safety.
Ana	Russian from Greek	She who will rise again.
Anabelle	Latin	Lovable
Anahid	Armenian	Goddess of the Moon
Anais		Pure, chaste.
Anamika	Hindu	
Anan	Arabic	Of the, clouds.
Anana	African	Soft, gentle.
Ananda	Sanskrit	Joyful.
Anani	Hawaiian	Orange tree.
Anar	Hindu	
Anastasia	Russian from Greek	She who will rise again. The name of a 4th-century saint.
Anata	Babylonian	The goddess of the Earth.
Anatola	Greek	From the East.
Anaya	Latin	
Anca		Grace, or favored by God. From the Hebrew name Hannah, meaning.
Ancelin	Old French	A spear attendant. The feminine form of Lancelot.
Anchoret		Free from shame, or much loved.
Ancika	Hebrew	Grace, or favored by God. From the Hebrew name Hannah, meaning.
Ancilla	Latin	A handmaiden.
Andea	Latin	A woman of the Andes.
Andie		Strong. The feminine form of Andrew or Andreas.
Andras	Norwegian	Breath.
Andraya		Trusted by God, royalty.

Andrea	Greek	Strong. The feminine form of Andrew or Andreas.
Andreana	Latin	Womanly.
Andria	Italian	Love, joy.
Andromache	Greek/Teutonic	From Shakespeare's play Troilus & Cressida.
Andromeda	Greek	A ruler of men. A heroine of Greek legend, who was rescued from a sea monster by Perseus.
Andy		Strong. The feminine form of Andrew or Andreas.
Aneira	Welsh	Truly golden. The feminine form of Aneurin.
Anemone	Greek	A wind flower. A mythological nymph who turned into a flower.
Aneya		
Anezka	Czech	Pure, chaste. Form of Agnes.
Angela	Greek	A heavenly messenger, an angel. Also see Angelica.
Angelica	Latin	The angelic one. Also a form of Angela and a plant name.
Angeni	Native American	Spirit angel.
Angevin	French	Angel of wine.
Angharad	Welsh	Free from shame, or much loved.
Angwen	Welsh	Very handsome.
Aniela	Italian/Polish	A heavenly messenger, an angel. Form of Angela.
Anika		Very beautiful.
Anila	Sanskrit	Of the wind.
Anisa	Arabic	Friendly.
Anita		Grace, or favored by God.
Anitra		A name created by Norwegian playwright Henrik Ibsen for his play Peer Gynt.
Anja		
Anjali	Hindu	
Anjana	Hindu	
Anka	Aboriginal	A barramundi.
Ankareeda	Aboriginal	Night star, graceful, shining.
Anke	Hebrew	Grace.
Ankita	Hindu	
Ann		Grace, or favored by God.

Ann-Margret		From Anne and Margaret. Anne - Grace, or favored by God. Margaret - A pearl.
Anna		Grace, or favored by God.
Annabel		Combination of Anna (grace) and Belle (beautiful).
Annabeth		
Annalise		Gracious and consecrated to God.
Annalynn		
Annamaria		Grace, or favored by God.
Annapurna	Hindu	A Hindu Goddesses.
Annata	Italian	Grace, or favored by God. Form of Anne.
Anne		Grace, or favored by God.
Anneliese	German/Scandinavian	From Anne and Liese. Anne - Grace, or favored by God. Liese - Consecrated to God.
Annette		Grace, or favored by God.
Annice	Old English	Pure, chaste. Form of Agnes.
Annika		Grace, or favored by God.
Anninka		Grace, or favored by God.
Annissa	Arabic	Charming, gracious.
Annora	Latin	Honor.
Annunziata	Italian	The bearer of news.
Anona	Latin	Of the harvest.
Anoush	Armenian	Sweet.
Anselma	Teutonic	A divine helmet. The feminine form of Anselm.
Anshu	Hindu	
Anstice	Russian from Greek	The resurrected one.
Anteia	Greek	A mythological figure.
Anthea	Greek	Flower-like.
Antigone	Greek	A name featured in mythology and implying strength of character.
Antionette	Latin	Flourishing, praiseworthy. From the name Antonia.
Antje	German	Grace.
Antoinette		Beyond price, praiseworthy. The feminine form of Antony.
Antonia	Latin	Beyond price, praiseworthy. The feminine form of Antony.

Antonie		Worthy of praise. Feminine form of Anthony.
Anupama	Hindu	
Anuradha	Hindu	A bright star.
Anusia	Greek/Polish	Grace, or favored by God.
Anusree	Hindu	Pretty, beautiful.
Anvita	Hindu	
Anya		Grace, or favored by God.
Anzu	Japanese	An apricot.
Aolani	Hawaiian	A heavenly cloud.
Apanie	Aboriginal	Water.
Apara	Nigerian	One who comes and goes.
Aparajita	Hindu	
Aparna	Hindu	Same as Parvati.
Aphra	Hebrew	Dust.
Aphrodite	Greek	The mythological goddess of beauty, love and fertility.
Apirka	Gaelic	Pleasant.
Apolline	Greek	The sun, sunlight.
Apollonia	Greek	Belonging to Apollo.
Aponi	Native American	Butterfly.
April	Latin	From April, the first month in the Roman calendar, and the beginning of Spring.
Aqua	Latin	A gemstone and color name. From the name Aquamarine.
Aquamarine	Latin	A color name.
Aquaria	Latin	After the zodiac sign and constellation of Aquarius.
Aquene	Native American	Peace.
Arabella	Latin	A beautiful altar.
Arabelle	German	Beautiful eagle.
Araceli	Latin	Alter of heaven.
Arachne	Greek	A mythological maiden who was turned into a spider.
Araluen	Aboriginal	The place of waterlilies.
Araminta	Greek	A beautiful, fragrant flower.
Arashel	Hebrew	Strong and protected hill.
Araxie	Armenian	River said to inspire poetic expression.
Arcadia	Greek	After Arcady, a mountainous region of Greece.

Arda	Armenian	
Ardath	Hebrew	A field of flowers.
Ardelia	Latin	Zealous.
Ardelle	Latin	Warm and enthusiastic.
Arden	Old English/Latin	Old English: A dwelling place. Latin: Ardent and sincere.
Ardere	Latin	Fire, fury.
Ardine		Warm and enthusiastic.
Ardis		Warm and enthusiastic.
Arella	Hebrew	Angel messenger.
Areta	Greek	Virtuous, one of untarnished reputation.
Aretha	Greek	The best, nymph.
Aretina	Greek	Virtuous.
Arezou	Persian	Wishful.
Argenta	Latin	The silvery one.
Aria	Latin	A beautiful melody.
Ariadne	Greek	The holy one.
Ariana		Like a beautiful melody.
Ariane		The holy one.
Aricia	Greek	Princess of the royal blood of Athens.
Ariella	Hebrew	God's lioness.
Arielle		Ethereal.
Ariene	Welsh	Silvery.
Arika	Aboriginal	A waterlily.
Arilda	German	A hearth maiden.
Arinya	Aboriginal	A kangaroo.
Arista	Greek	The best.
Ariza	Hebrew	A Cedar tree.
Arlene		A modern name of uncertain origin.
Arlette	Teutonic	An eagle.
Arlynda		Pledge.
Armada	Spanish	The armed one.
Armelle	French/Celtic	A princess.
Armilla	Latin	A bracelet.
Armina	Teutonic	A warrior maid. The feminine form of Herman.
Armorel		Gaelic the one who lives by the sea.

Armynel	French	A woman of the army. The feminine form of Armand.
Arnalda	Teutonic	Strong as an eagle. Feminine form of Arnold.
Arnisha		
Arnurna	Aboriginal	A blue waterlily.
Aroha	Maori	Love.
Arora	Aboriginal	A cockatoo.
Arran		The name of a Scottish island.
Artemis	Greek	Perfect. The name of the Greek goddess of the moon and hunting.
Artemisia	Greek	Belonging to Artemis.
Arti	Indonesian	A popular girl's name.
Aruna	Sanskrit	The dawn.
Arushi	Hindu	
Arva	Greek	An eagle.
Arziki	African Hausa	Prosperity.
Asa	Hebrew/Japansese	Hebrew: The healer, a physician. A biblical name. Japanese: The morning.
Asella		After St. Asella, who was described as `a flower of the Lord'.
Asenette	Hebrew	
Asenka	Hebrew	Graceful.
Asha	Sanskrit	Hope.
Ashamed	Hebrew	Ashes.
Ashima	Hindu	
Ashira	Hebrew	Wealthy.
Ashleigh	Old English	An Ash tree meadow or wood.
Ashley	Old English	From the Ash tree.
Ashling	Irish Gaelic	A vision or dream.
Ashrita	Hindu	
Asia	Greek	East.
Asisa	Hebrew	Ripe.
Askini	Hindu	Daughter of Prajapati Virat.
Asmara		An Ethiopian city.
Asmita	Hindu	Pride.
Aspasia	Greek	Welcome.
Aspen		

Assunta	Italian	From the Assumption of the Virgin Mary.
Asta	Greek/Old Norse	A star. Also a short form of Astrid.
Aster	Greek	After the flower.
Astera	Hebrew	Flower name.
Astra	Greek	Like a star.
Astrea	Greek	Innocence. The Greek goddess of justice, who left Earth and became a constellation.
Astrid	Old Norse	Divine strength.
Atalanta	Greek	The name of a swift runner in classical mythology.
Atara	Hebrew	A crown.
Atarah	Hebrew	A crown.
Athalia	Hebrew	God is exalted.
Athanasia	Greek	Immortal.
Athela	Old English	Noble.
Athena	Greek	A wise woman. After Athene, the Greek goddess of wisdom.
Atifa	Arabic	Affection.
Atin	Indonesian	A common girl's name.
Atiya	Arabic	A gift.
Atlanta	Greek	The name of a swift runner in classical mythology. Also a major city.
Atmaja	Hindu	Daughter.
Aubina		A white lady, someone of very fair hair and coloring.
Aubine		A white lady, someone of very fair hair and coloring.
Audlin		Pale.
Audora		
Audrey	Old English	Strong and noble, regal. A Shakespearean character in As You Like It.
Audun	Norwegian	Deserted.
Augusta	Latin	Majestic, or revered. The feminine form of Augustus.
Aundy	Norwegian	New prosperity.
Aura	Latin/Greek	Latin A gentle breeze. Greek of the air.
Aure	Greek	Breeze, soft-air.
Aurelia	Latin	Golden.

Aurkene	Basque	Presentation.
Aurora	Latin	Daybreak. The goddess of the dawn.
Ausiana		
Autumn	Latin	Autumn.
Ava	Greek	An eagle.
Avalon		The legendary island where King Arthur is supposedly buried. Also a Sydney location.
Avani	Hindu	
Avanti	Hindu	Ancient Malwa.
Avantika	Hindu	
Avara	Sanskrit	The youngest.
Avasa	Hindu	Independent.
Avel	Greek/Hebrew/Russian	Breath.
Aveline	Old French	From a location. Also see Evelyn.
Avena	Latin	From the Oat field.
Aveolela	Samoan	Rays of the sun.
Avera	Hebrew	A transgressor.
Averah		A transgressor.
Averil	Old English	The slayer of the boar.
Avery	Old English	The ruler of the elves.
Avice	French	Warlike.
Avis	Latin	A bird. Also a variation of Avice.
Aviva	Modern Jewish	Of the Springtime.
Avoca	Irish	A sweet valley.
Avril	French	From April, the first month in the Roman calendar, and the beginning of Spring. French form of April.
Awsta	Welsh	Majestic, or revered. The Welsh form of Augusta.
Awusi	Ghanian	Born on a Sunday.
Axelia	Greek	Protector of mankind.
Axelle	Teutonic	The father of peace. The feminine form of Axel.
Ayala	Modern Hebrew	A deer.
Ayame	Japanese	Iris.
Ayasha	Muslim	Mohamed's wife.
Ayelin	Ayla, Linn	
Ayesha		Life. The name of Mohamed's third and favorite wife.

Ayiana	American Indian	Eternal bloom.
Ayita	Native American	Worker.
Ayla	Hebrew	Oak tree.
Aylwen	Welsh	A fair brow.
Ayme		
Ayse	Turkish	
Aysegil	Turkish	
Ayushi	Hindu	
Ayushmati	Hindu	Person who has a long life.
Azadeh	Latin, Persian	Dry earth; detached, free of material things.
Azalea	Latin/Teutonic	Latin Dry: Earth. Teutonic Noble: Cheer. Also a flower name.
Azalia	Hebrew	Spared by Jehovah.
Azaria	Hebrew	Helped by God.
Azarni	Japanese	A thistle flower.
Aziza	Arabic	The cherished one.
Azland		
Azra	Arabic	Virginal.
Azrael		
Azura	Old French	From the Persian for blue sky.
Baako	African	First born.
Babette		The foreigner or stranger.
Bacia	Ugandan	Family deaths ruined the home.
Bageshwari	Hindu	
Baji		Joyful.
Baka	Hindu	Crane.
Bakana	Aboriginal	A lookout.
Bakarne	Basque	Solitude.
Bala	Sanskrit	A young girl.
Balbina	Latin	Strong, stammers.
Bambalina	Italian	Little girl.
Bambi		Child.
Banan	Arabic	Fingertips.
Bansari	Hindu	
Bara	Hebrew	To choose.
Barakah	Arabic	White one.
Barb	Latin	The foreigner or stranger. From the name Barbara.
Barbara	Latin	The foreigner or stranger.

Barbie	Latin	The foreigner or stranger. From the name Barbara.
Bari	French, Celtic, Welsh	Spear thrower, son of Harry, marksman.
Barika	Swahili	Successful.
Barina	Aboriginal	The summit.
Barnadine		Bold as a bear. From the name Bernard.
Barretta	unknown	A cap.
Basha	Hebrew, Greek, Polish	Daughter of God, stranger.
Basia	Polish	The foreigner or stranger.
Basilia	Greek	Queenly, regal. The feminine form of Basil.
Basimah	Arabic/Russian	The smiling one.
Bates		
Bathilde	Teutonic	The commanding maiden of war.
Bathsheba	Hebrew	The daughter of the oath, or the seventh daughter. The wife of King David in the Bible.
Batyah	Modern Hebrew	The daughter of God.
Bayo	Nigerian	To find joy.
Beata	Latin	Blessed.
Beatrice	Latin	The blessed one. She who brings joy. Beatrix was the name of a 4th-century saint.
Beatriz		Blessed.
Beau	French	Handsome or beautiful.
Bebe	French	Baby.
Beccalynn	English	
Beckie		A heifer or a knotted cord.
Becky		A heifer or a knotted cord.
Beda	Old English	A warrior maiden.
Bedelia	Old English	Strength.
Bega	Aboriginal	Beautiful. A town in New South Wales.
Begonia		A flower name.
Behira	Hebrew	The brilliant one.
Bel	Hindu	Sacred wood apple tree.
Bela	Hungarian	The white one.
Belda	French	A beautiful lady.
Belicia	Spanish	Dedicated to God.
Belina	French	A goddess.

Belinda	Italian	Beautiful.
Belita	Spanish	The beautiful one.
Belladonna	Italian	Beautiful woman.
Bellanca	Greek	Stronghold.
Belle	French	Beautiful.
Bellona	Latin	After the Roman goddess of war.
Belva		Beautiful.
Belvia		Beautiful.
Benedicta	Latin	Blessed. The feminine form of Benedict.
Benilda	Latin	Benign, of good intentions.
Benita	Latin	Daughter of my right hand. Feminine form of Benedict.
Benquasha	Native American	daughter of Ben
Benta	Hebrew	The wise one.
Beranger	French	Courage of a bear.
Berdine	Teutonic	A glorious maiden.
Berenice	Greek	The bringer of victory.
Berit	Old German	Bright, glorious.
Bernadette	French from Teutonic	As brave as a bear. The feminine form of Bernard. Generally a Catholic name.
Bernadine		Bold as a bear. From the name Bernard.
Bernia	Old English	A maiden of battle.
Bernice		Brings victory.
Bernina		After a peak in the Swiss Alps.
Berry	Old English	A fruit or berry.
Berta		A bright or famous pledge. The feminine form of Gilbert.
Bertana	Aboriginal	The day.
Bertha	Teutonic	Bright and shining. Also see Roberta.
Berthilda	Old English	A shining warrior maid.
Berwyn	Welsh	Fair-haired, or a bright friend.
Beryan	Cornish	The name of a saint.
Beryl	Greek	A precious green jewel.
Bess		Consecrated to God. Also see Isabel and Lisa.
Bessie		Consecrated to God.
Bessy		Consecrated to God.
Beta	Czech	Dedicated to God.

Beth	Hebrew	house of god
Bethan	Welsh	A form of Elizabeth, meaning consecrated to God.
Bethany	Hebrew	A house of poverty. A location from the New Testament.
Bethel	Hebrew	The house of God.
Bethesda	Hebrew	A house of mercy. A place mentioned in the Bible.
Bethia	Hebrew	The daughter of God.
Bethshaya	English	
Betrys	Welsh	The blessed one. She who brings joy. Form of Beatrice.
Betsey		A form of Elizabeth, meaning consecrated to God.
Betsy		A form of Elizabeth, meaning consecrated to God.
Bette		Consecrated to God.
Bettie		Consecrated to God.
Bettina		Consecrated to God.
Betty		Consecrated to God.
Beulah	Hebrew	The married one. Also a biblical location.
Beverley	Old English	From the stream of the beaver. Originally derived from a surname.
Beverly	Old English	From the stream of the beaver.
Bevin	Irish Gaelic	Sweet voiced, melodious.
Bharati	Hindu	
Bhavya	Hindu	
Bhayana	Hindu	
Bhoomi	Hindu	Earth.
Bian	Vietnamese	Secretive, or hidden.
Bianca	Italian	Fair-haired, or of a fair complexion. Form of Blanche. Used by Shakespeare for characters in two of his plays.
Bibi	Arabic	A lady.
Biddy	Irish	Strong, spirited. An ancient Celtic goddess. From the name Bridget.
Bijal	Hindu	

Billie	Teutonic	A wise ruler or protector. Feminine form of Billy and William, and also a diminutive of Wilhelmina.
Bina	Hebrew	Intelligence, understanding. Also a Diminutive of Sabina.
Binda	Aboriginal	Deep water.
Bindiya	Hindu	
Binty	Swahili	Daughter.
Birdie	Modern English	A little bird.
Birget	Norwegian	Protecting.
Birgit	Scandinavian	Strong, spirited. An ancient Celtic goddess. Form of Bridget.
Birgitta	Scandinavian	Strong, spirited. An ancient Celtic goddess. Form of Bridget.
Birgitte	Scandinavian	Strong, spirited. An ancient Celtic goddess. Form of Bridget.
Birkita	Celtic	Strength.
Blaine	Irish Gaelic	Thin.
Blair	Scottish Gaelic	From the plain or field.
Blaise	Latin	One who lisps or stammers.
Blake	Old English	Fair-haired.
Blanche	Old French	Fair-haired, or of a fair complexion.
Blanda	Teutonic	Dazzling.
Blaze		A flame.
Blenda		Beautiful. From the name Belinda.
Blinda		Beautiful. From the name Belinda.
Blinn		
Bliss	Old English	Joy, gladness.
Blodwen	Welsh	White flower, or blessed flower.
Blondelle	French	The little blond or fair one.
Blossom	Old English	A flower or bloom.
Bluma	Old German	A flower or bloom.
Bly	Native American	High, tall.
Blythe	Old English	Joyous and cheerful.
Bo	Old Norse/Chinese	Old Norse: A householder. Chinese: Precious.
Bo-Bae	Korean	Treasure, precious.
Boa		
Bobbi		Bright fame, famous. Feminine form of Robert. Also see Robin.

Bobbie	Teutonic	Famous, bright fame.
Bobby	Teutonic	Famous, bright fame.
Bodil	Old Norse	A battle maiden.
Bohdana	Russian	From God.
Bona	Latin	Good.
Bonita	Spanish	Pretty.
Bonnie	English/Scottish	Fine, pretty. Also see Bonita.
Bonny	English/Scottish	Fine, pretty. Also see Bonita.
Borgny	Norwegian	Help, new.
Boronia		A plant name.
Bracha	Hebrew	A blessing.
Brandee		Brandy, after dinner drink.
Brandi	beacon light	
Brandie	Dutch	Brandy, fine wine.
Brandy	Dutch	Brandy, fine wine. Also a feminine form of Brandon.
Branka	Slovenian	
Branwen	Welsh	Beautiful, or a holy raven.
Breda		A city in the Netherlands.
Bree		Strong, spirited. An ancient Celtic goddess.
Brenda	Old Norse	A flaming sword.
Brenna	Irish Gaelic	Raven-haired.
Bretta	Celtic	From Britain
Briallen	Welsh	A Primrose.
Briana	Celtic	Noble, honorable. The feminine form of Brian.
Brianna		Noble, honorable. The feminine form of Brian.
Brianne		Noble, honorable. The feminine form of Brian.
Briar	Middle English	A thorny plant.
Bridget	Irish Gaelic	Strong, spirited. An ancient Celtic goddess. St Brigid is one of Ireland's patron saints.
Brie		Strong, spirited. An ancient Celtic goddess. From the name Bridget and Briana, but also an independent name.
Brier	French	Heather.
Brietta	Celtic	Strong.
Brigit		Strong.

Brigitte	French/German	Strong, spirited. An ancient Celtic goddess. From the name Bridget.
Brilynn		Strength, cascade.
Brina	Celtic	Protector.
Briony		A vine-like plant.
Brit		From the name Britannia.
Britany		From the name Brittania.
Brites	Celtic	Strength.
Britt		A Swedish form of Bridget.
Brittania		From Brittain, British.
Brittany	Latin	Britain. Also the name of a French province.
Brittnee		From Britain.
Brodie	Irish Gaelic	A ditch.
Bron	African	The source.
Brona	Irish	Sorrow.
Bronnen	Cornish	A rush.
Bronte	English	From the surname of the Bronte sisters, novelists Anne, Charlotte and Emily.
Bronwen	Welsh	White or fair breasted.
Bronwyn	Welsh	Fair breast.
Bronya	Slavonic	Armour, protection.
Brook	Old English	At the brook or stream.
Brooke	Old English	At the brook or stream.
Bruna	Teutonic	Brown, or dark-haired. The feminine form of the boy's name Bruno. Also see Bruella.
Brunella	Teutonic/Italian	Brown-haired.
Brunhilde	Teutonic	An armed warrior maiden. The name given to a warrior queen in Germanic legend.
Bryanne		Strong one.
Brygid	Polish	Strength.
Brygida		Irish Gaelic: Strong, spirited. An ancient. Celtic: Goddess. St Brigid is one of Ireland's patron saints.
Bryher	Celtic	The name of one of the Scilly Isles, off the coast of Cornwall.
Bryn	Welsh	A hill.
Bryna	Irish	Strength.

Name	Origin	Meaning
Bryony	Greek	A vine-like plant.
Brysen		
Buena	Spanish	Good.
Buffy		A form of Elizabeth, meaning consecrated to God.
Bunny	English	A little rabbit.
Bunty	English	Originally used as a pet count, perhaps meaning a lamb.
Burdette		Courageous.
Burilda	Aboriginal	A black swan.
Buttercup		A flower name.
Butterfly		A butterfly.
Cade		Pure.
Cadee		Pure.
Cadence	Latin	Rhythmic.
Cadrian	Rhian	
Caelyn		Loved forever.
Cai	Vietnamese	
Cailey		
Cailin	Gaelic	A girl.
Caimile	African	A family is born.
Cairine	Gaelic	Pure. From the name Catherine or Katherine.
Cairistiona	Scottish Gaelic	A follower of Christ, a Christian.
Cait	Irish Gaelic	Pure, virginal.
Caitlin	Irish Gaelic	Pure. From the name Catherine or Katherine.
Caitlyn		Pure. From the name Catherine or Katherine.
Caitrin	Irish Gaelic	Pure. From the name Catherine or Katherine.
Caja	Cornish	A daisy.
Cala	Arabic	Castle.
Calandra	Greek	A lark.
Calantha	Greek	A beautiful blossom.
Caledonia	Latin	A woman from Scotland.
Calendre	Greek	
Caley	Irish Gaelic	Slender.
Calida	Latin	Warns and loving.
Calista	Greek	The most beautiful one.
Calix		Very handsome.

Calixte		Very beautiful.
Calla	Greek	Beautiful.
Callan	German	Chatter.
Callia	French	Beautiful.
Callidora	Greek	The gift of beauty.
Calliope	Greek	A beautiful voice. The muse of poetry in Greek mythology.
Callista		Most beautiful.
Callisto	Greek/Latin	Greek: A mythological nymph. Latin: The beautiful little one.
Caltha	Latin	Yellow flower.
Calypso	Greek	A legendary sea nymph. Also a West Indian style of music.
Cam	Vietnamese, English	Orange fruit, sweet, beloved, referring to the sun.
Cambria	Latin	An ancient name for Wales.
Camelai	Latin	A flower name.
Camellia		A flower name.
Cameo	Italian	An engraved gem.
Camilla	Latin	From a Roman family name, possibly meaning noble.
Camille	Latin	Virginal, unblemished character. Also from a Roman family name.
Camira	Aboriginal	Of the wind.
Canace	Greek	The daughter of the wind.
Candace	English/Latin	Possibly meaning brilliant white or clarity. The name of several queens of Ethiopia, and mentioned in the Bible.
Candice		Possibly meaning brilliant white or clarity. From the name Candace.
Candida	Latin	White.
Candide		Dazzling white.
Candie		Possibly meaning brilliant white From the name Candace.
Candra	Latin	Luminescent.
Candy	English	The sweet one. Also a nickname from Candace and Candida.
Cantara	Arabic	Small bridge.
Caoimhe	Celtic	Gentleness, beauty, grace.
Capri		Italian island.

Caprice	Italian	Unpredictable, whimsical.
Cara	Irish Gaelic/Cornish/Italian	Irish Gaelic: A friend. Cornish: Love. Italian: The beloved one.
Caragh	Irish	Love.
Carajean		Sweet melody.
Caralee		From Cara and Lee. Cara - Irish Gaelic: A friend. Cornish: Love. Italian: The beloved one. Lee - A meadow or a clearing.
Caralyn		From Cara and Lynn. Cara - Irish Gaelic: A friend. Cornish: Love. Italian: The beloved one. Lynn - A waterfall.
Cardinia	Aboriginal	The dawn.
Caren		Pure. Also see Catherine, Karen and Kathleen.
Carensa		Love.
Carenza		Love.
Caresse		Beloved.
Carew	Latin	Run.
Carey	Irish/Celtic/Cornish	Irish: The name of a castle. Celtic: From the river. Cornish: The loved one.
Carha		A pillar stone.
Cari	Turkish	Flows like water.
Carin	Irish Gaelic/Cornish/Italian	Irish Gaelic: A friend. Cornish: Love. Italian: The beloved one.
Carina	Aboriginal	A bride. Also see Cara.
Carine		Irish Gaelic: A friend. Cornish: Love. Italian: The beloved one.
Carissa	Latin	The most beloved one.
Carla		A free person. A feminine form of Charles, Also see Carla, Carol and Caroline.
Carleigh	German	Freeholder.
Carlen	Teutonic	Woman.
Carlie		A free person. A feminine form of Charles, Also see Carla, Carol and Caroline.
Carlin	Cornish/IrishGaelic	Cornish: From the fort by the pool. Irish Gaelic: The little champion.
Carlina	Italian	A free person.
Carling	Old English	Hill where old women or witches gather.

Carlota		A free person. A feminine form of Charles, Also see Carla, Carol and Caroline.
Carlotta		A free person. A feminine form of Charles, Also see Carla, Carol and Caroline.
Carly		A free person. A feminine form of Charles, Also see Carla, Carol and Caroline.
Carmel	Hebrew	A garden or orchard.
Carmela	Italian	A garden or orchard.
Carmelita	Spanish	A garden or orchard.
Carmen	Spanish	A garden or orchard.
Carmine		A garden or orchard.
Carmita		A garden or orchard.
Carna	Arabic	Horn.
Carnation		A flower name.
Carnelian		The name of a gemstone.
Carol		A free person.
Carolena		Little and womanly.
Caroline		A free person. A feminine form of Charles, Also see Carla, Carol and Caroline.
Carolyn		From the name Carol and Linda. Carol - A free person. Lyn - A waterfall.
Caron	French	Pure.
Carreen	English	A character in Margaret Mitchell's Gone With the Wind. Also see Cara.
Carrie	English	A free person.
Carrieann		Gracious and womanly.
Carrigan	Gaelic	
Carrington	Old English	Beautiful.
Carryl	Welsh	Love. Also see Carol.
Cary	Irish/Celtic/Cornish	Irish: The name of a castle. Celtic: From the river. Cornish: The loved one.
Caryn	Irish Gaelic/Cornish/Italian	Irish Gaelic: A friend. Cornish: Love. Italian: The beloved one.
Carys	Welsh	The beloved one.
Cascadia	Greek	Falling.
Casey	Irish Gaelic	The vigilant one.
Casilda	Latin	Of the home.

Casondra		Not to be believed.
Cassandra	Greek	In legend, a Trojan princess with the gift of prophecy.
Cassia	Hebrew	From the Cassia tree, a variety of cinnamon. Also see Kezia.
Cassiel	Latin	Angel of Saturday, the Earthy mother.
Casta	Latin	Pure and modest.
Castalia	Greek	A mythological figure.
Catalin		Wizard.
Catalina	Spanish	Pure. From the name Catherine or Katherine. Also used as an independent name.
Catalonia	Spanish	A region of Spain.
Catarina	Portuguese	Pure. From the name Catherine or Katherine.
Catava	African	Name from a proverb.
Caterina	Italian	Pure. From the name Catherine or Katherine.
Cathay		An archaic name for China.
Cathee		Pure. From the name Catherine or Katherine.
Catherine	Greek	Pure. From the name Catherine or Katherine.
Cathie		Pure. From the name Catherine or Katherine.
Cathleen	Irish	Pure, virginal. Also see Catherine.
Cathlene	Irish	Pure, virginal. Also see Catherine.
Cathy		Pure. From the name Catherine or Katherine.
Catrin	Welsh	Pure. From the name Catherine or Katherine.
Catriona	Gaelic	Pure. From the name Catherine or Katherine.
Cauvery	Hindu	Cavery.
Cayla		Pure. From the name Catherine or Katherine.
Cayleigh	Gaelic	Party.
Ceana		God is gracious.
Cecania	German	Free.
Cecia	Seesha, Sessi	
Cecile		Blind.

Cecilia	Latin	The blind one, or the sixth. The feminine form of Cecil. Also see Sheila.
Cecily	Irish	The blind one, or the sixth. .
Ceinwen	Welsh	Blessed and fair.
Celandia	Greek	The swallow.
Celandine		A flower name.
Celena	Greek	The goddess of the moon.
Celene	Greek	The goddess of the moon.
Celeste	Latin	Heavenly.
Celestyn	Polish	Heaven.
Celia		The blind one, or the sixth. The feminine form of Cecil. Also see Sheila.
Celie	French	The blind one, or the sixth. The feminine form of Cecil. Also see Sheila.
Celina	Greek	The goddess of the moon.
Celine	Greek	The goddess of the moon.
Cerdwin	Celtic	The mother Goddess.
Cerelia	Latin	Of the spring
Ceres	Latin	The Roman goddess of corn and tillage.
Ceridwen	Welsh	Fair poetry.
Cerise	French	Cherry red.
Chaitaly	Hindu	
Chaitra	Hindu	Aries sign.
Chalsie		Seaport.
Chana		Gracious.
Chanah	Hebrew	Grace.
Chance	Old French	A church official or chancellor.
Chandani	Sanskrit	Name of the goddess Devi.
Chandi	Sanskrit	Name of the angry goddess Sakti.
Chandra	Sanskrit	A shining moon.
Chane	Hindu, Swahili	name of a god, dependability
Chanel	French	The name of a famous perfume.
Chantal	French	From a family name meaning stone or boulder.
Chantel		Rocky land or singer.
Charis	Greek	Grace, the graceful one.
Charisma	Greek	Grace, the graceful one.

Charissa	Greek	Grace, the graceful one.
Charisse		Grace, beauty, kindness.
Charity	Latin	Loving and benevolent. One of the three Graces in Greek mythology.
Charla		Womanly, full grown. Also see Carla, Carol and Caroline.
Charlee		Womanly, full grown. Also see Carla, Carol and Caroline.
Charleen		A free person. A feminine form of Charles, Also see Carla, Carol and Caroline.
Charleigh		Man.
Charlene		A free person. A feminine form of Charles, Also see Carla, Carol and Caroline.
Charline		Womanly, full grown.
Charlot		Womanly, full grown.
Charlotte		Womanly, full grown.
Charmaine	Greek	Delightful.
Charmian	Latin	From Shakespeare's play Antony & Cleopatra.
Charo		A free person. From the name Carol.
Charu	Hindu	
Chastity	Latin	Pure and chaste.
Chavi		Female child.
Chay	Old German	Man.
Chaya	Hebrew	Life.
Chaylen		
Chelle		Like the Lord. A feminine form of Michael.
Chelsa		Harbor.
Chelsea		From the name of a fashionable London suburb.
Chelsi		Seaport.
Chelsia		Harbor.
Chenoa	Native American	A white dove.
Cher	French	The beloved one.
Cheri		The beloved one.
Cherie		Beloved.

Cherilyn	English	Derived from Cher or Cheryl and Lynn. Cher and Cheryl - The beloved one. Lynn - A Waterfall.
Cherise	Greek	Grace.
Cherish	Old French	The treasured one.
Cherlin		The beloved one.
Cherry		The beloved one. Also a fruit name.
Cheryl		The beloved one.
Chesna	Slavonic	Peaceful.
Chevonne	Irish Gaelic	Form of Jane and Judith. Jane - God is gracious. Judith - A woman from Judea.
Chhavvi	Hindu	
Chhaya	Hindu	Shadow.
Chiara	Italian	Bright and famous. The name of an Irish county. Also See Clarice.
Chika	Japanese	Near.
Chilali	Native American	Snowbird.
Chimalis	Native American	Bluebird.
Chipo	African	Gift.
Chiquita	Spanish	The little one.
Chitra	Hindu	Portrait.
Chitrangda	Hindu	
Chizu	Japanese	A thousand storks. A name which implies longevity.
Chloe	Greek	A fertile young maiden.
Chloris	Greek	A plant lover.
Cho	Japanese/Korean	A butterfly. Korean beautiful.
Choden	Tibetan/Sherpa	The devout one.
Chow	Chinese	Summer.
Chrissy		Bearing Christ. From the name Christopher.
Christa		Bearing Christ.
Christabel	English	Beautiful Christian. Derived from Christina and Belle.
Christal		Clear as ice. A gemstone name.
Christea		Bearing Christ.
Christel		Clear as ice. A gemstone name.
Christelle		Clear as ice. A gemstone name.
Christian	Latin	A follower of Christ. A Christian.
Christiana		Christian, anointed.

Christie	Irish/Scottish	A follower of Christ, a Christian.
Christina	Latin	A follower of Christ, a Christian.
Christine		Bearing Christ. From the name Christopher.
Christmas	Old English	Born at Christmas time.
Christy	Irish/Scottish	A follower of Christ, a Christian.
Chruse	Greek	Golden, the golden one.
Chrysantha		A flower name. From Chrysanthemum - Greek for a golden flower.
Chrysilla	Greek	Golden-haired.
Chyou	Chinese	Autumn.
Ciannait	Irish	Ancient.
Ciar	Irish	Saint's name.
Ciara	Irish Gaelic	A spear.
Cicely		The blind one, or the sixth. The feminine form of Cecil. Also see Sheila.
Cicily		The blind one, or the sixth.
Cilla		From a Roman family name. From the name Priscilla.
Cinderella	French	A maiden of the cinders or ashes.
Cindy		A maiden of the cinders or ashes.
Cindylou		A maiden of the cinders or ashes. From Cindy and Louise.
Cinnabar	Greek	Red. A color name and also the name of a mineral.
Cinnamon	Hebrew	A spice name.
Circe	Greek	Witch-goddess, seductive.
Cirea		
Cissy		The blind one, or the sixth. .
Claiborne	Old English	Born of the Earth.
Claire	French	Bright and famous. Also See Clarice.
Clara		Bright and famous. Also See Clarice.
Clarabelle	Latin/French	Bright and beautiful. From Clara and Belle.
Clare	Latin	Bright and famous. The name of an Irish county. Also See Clarice.
Clarice	Latin/French	The little brilliant one.
Clarinda		Bright and famous. Also See Clarice.

Clarine		Bright and famous. Also See Clarice.
Clarissa		Brilliant.
Claudia	Latin	The lame one. The feminine form of Claude.
Clematis	Greek	A climbing plant. A flower name.
Clemence	Latin	Mild, merciful.
Clementine		Merciful.
Cleo		Glory of the father. The queen of Egypt from 47-30 BC.
Cleomenes		From Shakespeare's play Winter's Tale.
Cleopatra	Greek	Glory of the father. The queen of Egypt from 47-30 BC.
Cleta		Glory of the father.
Cleva	Old English	From the cliff. Feminine form of Clive.
Cliantha	Greek	A glorious flower.
Clio	Greek	The glorious one. The muse of history in Greek mythology. Also see Cleopatra.
Clodagh	Irish	From the name of a river.
Clodia		The lame one. The feminine form of Claude.
Clorinda	Persian	Of renowned beauty.
Cloris		A plant lover.
Clotilda	Teutonic	Famous battle maiden.
Clove		A nail.
Clover	Old English	A flower name.
Clymene	Greek	Renowned.
Cochiti	Spanish	Forgotten.
Cody	Old English	A pillow or cushion.
Colenso	Cornish	From the dark pool.
Colette	French	The people's victory. The feminine form of Nicholas.
Colleen	Irish Gaelic	A girl.
Colletta		The people's victory. The feminine form of Nicholas.
Collette		The people's victory. The feminine form of Nicholas.
Columba	Latin	Dove-like. The name of a 6th-century Irish saint.
Columbia	Old English	A dove.

Columbine		A flower name. Also see Columba.
Concepcion	Latin/Spanish	Latin: The beginning. Spanish: A name that relates to the Virgin Mary's Immaculate Conception.
Concordia	Latin	The harmonious one.
Conncetta	Conny	
Connie		Steadfast, constant.
Constance	Latin	Steadfast, constant.
Consuela	Latin	The consoler or comforter.
Consuelo	Spanish	Consolation.
Coorah	Aboriginal	A woman.
Cora	Greek	A maiden.
Corabelle		A combination of Con and Belle, meaning a beautiful maiden.
Coral	Latin	From the sea.
Coralia	Greek	Like coral.
Coralie		Little maiden.
Corazon	Spanish	The heart. Often used in the Philippines.
Corbin		A raven.
Cordelia	Celtic	A jewel of the sea.
Coreen	Aboriginal	The end of the hills.
Corentine		Little Cora.
Corey	Celtic/Gaelic	Dweller in the hollow.
Corin	Cornish/Latin	Cornish: From the corner. Latin: The name of a Roman deity, possibly meaning a spear. Also from Shakespeare's play As You Like It.
Corina		A maiden.
Corinda		A maiden.
Corine		A maiden.
Corinna		A maiden.
Corinne		A maiden.
Corliss	Old English	The cheerful one.
Cornelia	Latin	A horn. The feminine form of Cornelius.
Cornelian		The name of a gemstone.
Corona	Latin	A town.
Corowa	Aboriginal	A rocky river.
Corrine		A maiden.

Cory		Helmet.
Cosette		Victorious people.
Cosima	Greek	Perfect order.
Cossette	French	Of the victorious.
Courtney	Old French	The short-nosed one, or from a location.
Crescent	Old French	One who creates, curved.
Cressida	Greek	The golden one. A Shakespearean character.
Crisiant	Welsh	Like a crystal.
Crispina	Latin	The curly-haired one. Feminine form of Crispin.
Cristin		A follower of Christ, a Christian.
Cristina		A follower of Christ, a Christian.
Cristine		A follower of Christ, a Christian.
Cristiona	Irish Gaelic	A follower of Christ, a Christian.
Cristy		Bearing Christ. From the name Christopher.
Crystal	Greek	Clear as ice. A gemstone name.
Curissa		
Cuyler	Celtic	Chapel.
Cybele	French	The prophetess. From Greek mythology.
Cybil		The prophetess. From Greek mythology.
Cybill		The prophetess. From Greek mythology.
Cynara	Greek	Thistle.
Cyndi		Of the moon.
Cynere	Greek	An artichoke or thistle.
Cynthia	Greek	Of the moon. An alternative name for the Greek moon goddess, Artemis.
Cypriana	Greek	A woman from Cyprus.
Cyprien	French	A woman from Cyprus.
Cyrena	Greek	A woman from Cyrene, an ancient Greek colony in North Africa.
Cyrene	Greek	name of a mythological nymph
Cyrilla	Greek	Lordly or proud one. Feminine form of Cyril.
Cytheria	Latin	Venus.
Cyzarine	Russian	Royalty.

Daba	Hebrew	kind words, bee swarm
Dabria	Latin	Name of an angel.
Dacey	Gaelic	The southerner.
Dacia	Greek	A woman from Dacia, an ancient European country.
Dacio	French	
Dade		
Dae	Korean	Greatness.
Daffodil	English from Greek	The asphodel. A flower name.
Dagmar	Old Norse	A maiden of the day, or glorious day.
Dagna	Old Norse	A new day.
Dagny	Norwegian	Day, brightness, new day, Dane's joy.
Dahlia	English	From the flower, named after the Swedish botanist, Dahl, or possibly author Roald Dahl.
Dai	Welsh/Japanese	Welsh: The beloved, the adored one. Japanese: Great.
Daisy	Old English	The day's eye. A flower name. Also a nickname from Margaret.
Dakin	Danish	Danish
Daksha	Hindu	
Dale	Teutonic/Old English	A valley dweller.
Dalia		A branch, bough.
Dalila	Swahili	Gentle.
Dallas	Celtic	Skilled, or from the field of water. Also a city in Texas.
Damalis	Greek	Gentle.
Damara	Greek	Gentle girl.
Damaris	Greek	Gentle. A New Testament name.
Dame	German	Lady.
Damiana	Greek	Tame, domesticated. The feminine form of Damian/Damon.
Damini	Hindu	Lightning.
Damita	Spanish	The little noble lady.
Damosel	Old English	A damsel, or young unmarried woman.
Dana	Old English/Czech	Old English: From Denmark. Czech: God is my judge.
Danae	Greek	The mother of Perseus in Greek mythology.

Dani		My judge.
Danica	Slavic	The morning star.
Daniela		God is my judge.
Danielle	Hebrew	God is my judge. The feminine form of Daniel.
Danika	Slavonic	The morning star.
Dannell		
Danniell		God is my judge.
Danu	Gaelic	The goddess of fruitfulness.
Danuta	Polish	A little deer. Also see Dana.
Daphne	Greek	The laurel. In Greek mythology, the name of a nymph who was transformed into a Laurel tree.
Dara	Irish Gaelic/Hebrew	Irish: A son of oak. Hebrew: Compassion, wisdom.
Daralis	Old English	Beloved.
Daray		Dark.
Darby	Irish Gaelic/Middle English	Irish Gaelic: Free from envy. Middle English: The deer settlement.
Darcie	Old French	An old Norman family name.
Daria	Greek	Wealthy. The feminine form of Darius.
Darinka	Slovenian	
Darlene	English from Old French	The little darling, the beloved one.
Darra	Gaelic, Farsi	Small great one, riches, wealth.
Darrelle	Old French	The beloved one. The feminine form of Darrell.
Darrene	English	The Great one. The feminine form of Darren.
Darri	Aboriginal	A track.
Dasha	Greek	Gift of God.
Davan	Irish	The beloved, the adored one. Feminine form of David.
Davida		The beloved, the adored one. Feminine form of David.
Davina	Hebrew	The beloved one. The feminine form of David. Also see Vida.
Davine	Hebrew	The loved.
Dawa	Tibetan/Sherpa	Born on a Monday.
Dawn	English	Daybreak, dawn.
Daya	Hebrew	Bird.

Dayla	Hebrew	To draw water, branch or bough.
Dayle		A valley dweller.
Deana		The divine one. The goddess of hunting and the moon in Roman mythology. Feminine form of Dean.
Deanna		The divine one. The goddess of hunting and the moon in Roman mythology. Feminine form of Dean.
Deanne		The divine one. The goddess of hunting and the moon in Roman mythology. Feminine form of Dean.
Debbie	Hebrew	The bee, an industrious woman.
Debby	Hebrew	The bee, an industrious woman.
Deborah	Hebrew	The bee, an industrious woman. A biblical name.
Debra	Hebrew	The bee, an industrious woman.
Dechen	Tibetan/Sherpa	Health and happiness.
Decima	Latin	The tenth.
Dee		
Deena	Hindu	
Deepali	Hindu	
Deepika	Hindu	A little light.
Deepti	Hindu	
Deeta		The lost one.
Deianira	Greek	Wife of Hercules.
Deidra		Sorrowful, wanderer.
Deiene	Basque	Religious holiday.
Deion		
Deiondre		Valley.
Deirdre	Celtic	Sorrow. The name of a character from Irish legend.
Deja	French	Before, prior.
Delanna	Italian	As soft as wool.
Delbin	Greek	Dolphin, flower name.
Delcine		Sweet.
Delfina		Dolphin.
Delia	Greek	A woman from the island of Delos. Also another name for Artemis, the Greek moon goddess.
Delicia	Latin	Delight.

Delila		Hair or poor.
Delilah	Hebrew	The beautiful temptress. The lover of Samson in the Bible.
Dell	English	From the dell or hollow.
Della	English	A woman from the island of Delos. Probably derived from Delia or Delilah and Ella. Also a diminutive of Adele and Adelaide.
Delma	Spanish	Of the sea.
Delphine	Latin	A woman from Delphi or a flower name.
Delta	Greek	The fourth, as in fourth child.
Delvene	Latin	A woman from Delphi or a flower name from delphinium.
Delvine	Latin	A woman from Delphi or a flower name from delphinium.
Delwyn	Old English/Welsh	Old English: A friend from the valley. Welsh: Neat and fair.
Delyth	Welsh	Neat and pretty.
Dembe	Ugandan	Peace.
Demelza	Cornish	From a location. The heroine of Winston Graham's Poldark novels.
Demetria	Greek	From the goddess of fertility.
Demi	Latin	Half. Also see Demetria.
Dena	Old English	From the valley. Feminine form of Dean.
Denise	French from Greek	A lover of wine. The feminine form of Denis/Dennis.
Dep	Vietnamese	Beautiful.
Derica		Beloved leader.
Derryth	Welsh	Of the oak.
Dervla	Irish Gaelic	The daughter of the poet.
Desana		Longed for, desired.
Desdemona	Greek	Ill-fated. A Shakespearean character murdered by her husband Othello.
Desiree	Latin	The desired one.
Desma	Greek	A pledge.
Despina	Greek	
Desta	Ethiopian	Happiness.
Destinee	French	Destiny.

Destry	French	War horse.
Deva		Celestial spirit.
Devaki	Hindu	Black, mother of Krishna.
Devi	Breton/Sanskrit	Breton: The beloved, the adored one. Sanskrit: Godlike, a goddess.
Devika	Sanskrit	A little goddess.
Devnet	Swedish	Home of the Danes.
Devona	Old English	From the county of Devon.
Devora	Jewish	The bee, an industrious woman.
Devorah	Jewish	The bee, an industrious woman.
Devore		The bee, an industrious woman.
Dextra	Latin	Skilful, dexterous. The feminine form of Dexter.
Dharmista	Hindu	
Diamanta	French from Latin	Adamant, like a diamond.
Diana	Latin	The divine one. The goddess of hunting and the moon in Roman mythology.
Diane	French	The divine one.
Dianne	French	The divine one.
Diantha	Greek	A divine flower.
Dianthe	Greek	Flower of the Gods.
Dido	Greek	The name of a queen of Carthage.
Didrika	Teutonic	The people's ruler.
Diella	Latin	Worshiper of God.
Dierdre	Celtic	Young girl, one who rages, broken-hearted.
Dietlinde	German	
Dieuwertje	unknown	
Diki	Tibetan/Sherpa	Healthy and wealthy.
Dikranouhi	Armenian	Queen.
Dilek	Turkish	
Dillian	Latin	Worshiped one.
Dilys	Welsh	True, steadfast.
Dimity	Greek	From the cotton material.
Dina	Irish Gaelic	From the name Dean. Latin: A soldier. Teutonic: Merciful.
Dinah	Hebrew	Judgment. A biblical name.

Dione	Greek	A lover of wine. From Dionysus, the mythological God of wine and drama.
Dionne		The divine one.
Dionyza	Latin	From Shakespeare's play Pericles.
Dirran	Arabic	
Disa	Greek	Double.
Dita		The lost one.
Diva	Latin	A goddess.
Divya	Hindu	Heavenly, brilliant.
Dixie	French	The tenth. Also a girl from the American south.
Dobrila	Slavonic	Kind, good.
Dodie	Hebrew	Beloved. Also see Dorothy.
Doe		A deer.
Dohna	Tibetan/Sherpa	A female deity.
Dolkar	Tibetan/Sherpa	The name of a Buddhist Goddess.
Dollie		The gift of God. Also see Dora and Theodora.
Dolly		The gift of God.
Dolores	Spanish	Sorrow, pain. Derived from the seven sorrows of the Virgin Mary.
Dominga	Spanish	Sunday.
Dominica	Latin	Belonging to the lord. The feminine form of Dominic.
Dominique	Latin	Of God.
Donalda	Scottish Gaelic	The ruler of the world. The feminine form of Donald.
Donata	Latin	Given by God, a gift.
Donella	Scottish Gaelic	The ruler of the world. The feminine form of Donald.
Donelle	Scottish Gaelic	The ruler of the world. The feminine form of Donald.
Donla	Irish Gaelic	The brown lady.
Donna	Italian	A lady. A short form of Madonna.
Dooriya	English	the sea
Dora	Greek	A gift. Originally a short form of Dorothy and Theodora, but now also used as an independent name.
Dorcas	Greek	A gazelle, a doe. Also see Tabitha.

Dore	French	Golden.
Doreen		A gift. Originally a short form of Dorothy and Theodora.
Doria	Greek	A location.
Dorinda	Greek	Gift of God, beautiful one.
Doris	Greek	A woman from Doria, or from the ocean. A Greek goddess of the sea.
Dorota	Greek, Spanish	God's gift.
Dorothea	Dutch	The gift of God.
Dorothy	Greek	The gift of God.
Dot		The gift of God.
Dotty		The gift of God.
Douce	French	Gentle, sweet.
Dova	Teutonic	Peace, a dove.
Dreama	Greek	Joyous music.
Drew	Celtic	Courageous.
Drina	Spanish	Helper and defender of mankind.
Drisana	Hindu	Daughter of the Sun.
Dristi	Hindu	Sight, a form of the Devi.
Druella	Teutonic	An elfin vision.
Drusilla	Latin	From an old Roman family name.
Druti	Hindu	
Duana	Irish Gaelic	A little dark maiden.
Duena	Spanish	A chaperone.
Dulce	Italian	Sweet.
Dulcea	Italian	Sweet.
Dulcie	Latin	Sweet.
Dulcina		Rose.
Dulcinea	Latin	Sweet.
Durga	Sanskrit	Unattainable. A mythological Hindu goddess.
Dusana	Czech	A spirit, a soul.
Dusty	English	Warrior. Feminine form of Dustin.
Dyan	Roman	The divine one. The goddess of hunting and the moon in Roman mythology.
Dyana	Roman	The divine one. The goddess of hunting and the moon in Roman mythology.
Dyani	Native American	A deer.
Dyanne	Greek	The divine one.

Dymphna	Irish Gaelic	A fawn.
Dyna	Greek	Powerful. Also see Dinah.
Dysis	Greek	Sunset.
Dysthe	Greek	
Eartha	Old English	Of the Earth.
Easter	Old English	From the holiday.
Ebba	Old English	From the rich fortress.
Ebere	African	Mercy.
Eberta	Teutonic	Bright, brilliant.
Ebony	Greek	A black wood.
Ebrel	Cornish	From April, the first month in the Roman calendar, and the beginning of spring. Cornish form of April.
Echo	Greek	A repeating round. The name of a nymph in Greek mythology.
Eda	Old English	Rich, prosperous.
Edalene		Noble, King.
Edaline		Noble, King.
Edana	Gaelic	Fiery.
Edda	Old English	Rich.
Edeline	German	Noble and kind.
Eden	Hebrew/Old English	Hebrew: The place of pleasure (from the Garden of Eden). Old English: A bear cub.
Edena	Hawaiian	Renewal, rejuvenation.
Edeva	Old English	A rich gift.
Edina		A prosperous friend. The feminine form of Edwin.
Edith	Old English	Prosperity, or a gift.
Edlyn	Old English	A noble maiden.
Edme	Scottish	Protector. A variation of Esme, and the feminine form of Edmund.
Edmonda	Old English	A rich protector. The feminine form of Edmund.
Edna	Hebrew	Renewal, rejuvenation.
Edolie	Old English	Noble.
Edrea	Old English	Prosperous, powerful.
Edria	Hebrew	Mighty.
Edwerdina	Old English	A prosperous guardian. The female form of Edward.

Edwina	Old English	A prosperous friend. The feminine form of Edwin.
Edythe		Prosperity, or a gift.
Eerin	Aboriginal	A small grey owl.
Effie		Of good reputation.
Effy		Of good reputation.
Efia	Ghanese	Born on Tuesday.
Efrosini	Hebrew	A fawn or a bird.
Efterpi	Greek	Pretty in face.
Egeria	Greek	A wise adviser.
Eglantine	Old French	A flower name.
Eiddwen	Welsh	The beloved fair one.
Eileen	Irish Gaelic	The light of the sun. The Irish form of Helen.
Eilis	Irish Gaelic	A form of Elizabeth, meaning consecrated to God.
Eir	Old Norse	The name of the goddess of healing.
Eira	Welsh	Snow.
Eirian	Welsh	Silver.
Eirwen	Welsh	As white as snow.
Eithne	Irish Gaelic	Ardent, fiery.
Ekala	Aboriginal	A lake.
Ekaterina	Russian	Pure. From the name Catherine or Katherine.
Ekta	Hindu	
Ela	Old English	Elfin, a fairy maiden. Also a diminutive of Eleanor, Elizabeth, Ellen and Helen.
Elaine	English	From the Old French form of Helen.
Elana		A tree.
Elanora	Aboriginal	A home by the sea.
Elata	Latin	Exalted, of high birth.
Elberta		Noble and illustrious. The feminine form of Albert.
Elbertina		Noble and illustrious.
Elbertine		Noble and illustrious.
Elda	Italian	A battle maiden.
Eldora	Spanish	The golden one.
Eleanor	Old French	The light of the sun. A form of Helen.
Electra	Greek	Brilliant.

Elena	Italian/Portuguese/Spanish	The light of the sun.
Eleni	Greek	The light of the sun.
Elenna		A tree.
Eleora	Hebrew	The lord is my light.
Elephteria		Freedom.
Eleri	Welsh	The name of a river.
Elexus	Latin	
Elfreda		Noble and ready. Feminine form of Alphonse.
Elga		The holy one.
Eliane	Latin	From the Greek word for sun.
Elida		The little winged one.
Elie		The light of the sun. A form of Helen.
Elina	Greek, Hindu	Pure, intelligent.
Elinor		The light of the sun. A form of Helen.
Elinore		The light of the sun. A form of Helen.
Eliora	Hebrew	God is my light.
Elisa	Spanish	Dedicated to God
Elisabeth	English	Consecrated to God.
Elise	French	Consecrated to God. Also see Isabel and Lisa.
Elisha	Hebrew	God is my salvation. The successor of Elijah in the Bible.
Eliska	Czech	Truthful.
Elissa	Greek	Consecrated to God. Also see Isabel and Lisa.
Elita	Old French	The little winged one or the chosen one.
Elizabeth	Hebrew	Consecrated to God. A name from the Bible. Also see Isabel and Lisa.
Elke		The defender, or helper of mankind. Form of Alexandra.
Ella	Old English	Elfin, a fairy maiden. Also a diminutive of Eleanor, Elizabeth, Ellen and Helen.
Ellamay		A combination of Ella and May.
Elle	French	She, a woman.
Ellema	African	Milking a cow.
Ellen		The light of the sun.

Elli		The light of the sun
Ellice	Greek	Jehovah is God. The feminine form of Elias.
Ellie		The light of the sun.
Ellin	Aboriginal	To move.
Ellinor		The light of the sun. A form of Helen.
Elly		The light of the sun.
Elma	Greek	Pleasant, amiable.
Elmas	Armenian	A diamond.
Elmira	Old English	Noble.
Elodia		Wealthy, prosperous.
Elodie		Wealthy, prosperous.
Eloise	Teutonic	Healthy.
Elouera	Aboriginal	From the pleasant place.
Elrica	German	The ruler of all.
Elsa		A form of Elizabeth, meaning consecrated to God.
Else	Hebrew	consecrated to god
Elsie		Consecrated to God. Also see Isabel and Lisa.
Elspeth		Consecrated to God. Also see Isabel and Lisa.
Eluned	Welsh	A waterfall.
Elvan	Turkish	
Elvina	Old English	The friend of the elves.
Elvira	Latin/Teutonic	Latin: The fair one. Teutonic: A true stranger.
Elysa		Consecrated to God. Also see Isabel and Lisa.
Elyse		Consecrated to God. Also see Isabel and Lisa.
Elyshia		The light of the sun.
Elysia	Latin	Blissful.
Elyssa		Consecrated to God.
Elzira	Portuguese	Form of Elizabeth, meaning consecrated to God.
Ema	Polynesian	Beloved.
Emalia	Latin	Flirt.
Emanuel		God is with us.
Emanuela	Hebrew	God is with us.
Emanuele		God in humankind.
Ember	Old English	Smoldering remains of a fire.

Emelda		A floret.
Emelia		Industrious.
Emer	Irish Gaelic	A traditional name.
Emerald		A gemstone name.
Emilia		Ambitious, industrious.
Emilie		Ambitious, industrious.
Emily	Teutonic	Industrious. Also see Amelia.
Emina	Latin	A noble or lofty maiden.
Emma	Teutonic	The healer of the universe.
Emmanuel	Hebrew	God is with us.
Emmanuelle	Hebrew	God is with us. Feminine form of Emmanuel.
Emmet	Old English	Industrious.
Emmett		Truth.
Emmuna	Hebrew	
Emmylou		From Emily and Louise. Emily - Industrious. Louise - A famous warrior maiden.
Emogen	Celtic/Latin	Celtic: A girl or maiden. Latin: The image of her mother.
Emogene	Celtic/Latin	Celtic: A girl or maiden. Latin: The image of her mother.
Ena	Irish Gaelic	Ardent.
Enda	Irish Gaelic	Bird-like.
Endocia	Greek	Of unquestionable reputation.
Endora	Hebrew	A fountain.
Engelberta	Teutonic	A bright angel.
Engracia	Spanish	Graceful.
Enid	Celtic	A pure soul.
Ennor	Cornish	From the boundary.
Enola	Native American	Magnolia.
Enora	Greek	Light.
Enrica	Italian/Spanish	The ruler of the home. A feminine form of Henry.
Enya	Irish	
Enye	Yiddish	Grace.
Enys	Celtic	From the island. Also see Innes.
Eranthe	Greek	A flower of Spring.
Erasma	Greek	amiable
Erena		Peace.
Erene		Peace.

Erianthe	Greek	Sweet as many flowers.
Erica	Old Norse	A powerful ruler. The feminine form of Eric.
Erika	German/Scandinavian	A powerful ruler. The feminine form of Eric.
Erin	Irish Gaelic	From Ireland.
Eris	Greek	The goddess of discord.
Erlina	Celtic	Girl from Ireland.
Erline	Old English	A noblewoman. The feminine form of Earl.
Erma	Teutonic	A maiden of the army. The feminine form of Herman.
Ermine	Old French	From the name of the fur.
Ernestine	Teutonic	Serious, earnest. The feminine form of Ernest.
Erwina	Teutonic	An honorable friend.
Eryn	Irish Gaelic	From Ireland.
Erzsebet	Hebrew	Devoted to God
Eskarne	Spanish	Merciful.
Esme		Protector. The feminine form of Edmund.
Esmeralda	Spanish	Spanish expression meaning Emerald.
Esmerelda		Protector. The feminine form of Edmund.
Esperance	Latin	Hope.
Esperanza	Spanish	Hope.
Esta	Italian	From the East.
Estefania	Spanish	A garland or crown. The feminine form of Stephen.
Estelle	French from Latin	A star. Also see Esther and Stella.
Ester	Spanish	A star.
Esther	Hebrew	A star.
Etain	Irish	Shining, bright.
Etana	Hebrew	Determination.
Etania	Native American	Wealthy.
Eternity		Everlasting.
Ethel	Teutonic	A noble maiden.
Ethelda		Noble in counsel.
Etienette	French from Greek	A garland or crown. Feminine form of Etienne.
Etsu	Japanese	Delight.

Etta		The ruler of the home. A feminine form of Henry.
Ettie		The ruler of the home. A feminine form of Henry.
Euclea	Greek	Glory.
Eudocia		Of unquestionable reputation.
Eudocie		Of unquestionable reputation.
Eudora	Greek	A wonderful gift.
Eugenia	Greek	Noble, well-born. The feminine form of Eugene.
Eulalia	Greek	The well-spoken one.
Euna	Scottish	Also see Juno.
Eunice	Greek	Victorious.
Euphemia	Greek	Of good reputation.
Euphrasia	Greek	Joy, delight.
Euphrosyne	Greek	Joy.
Eurwen	Welsh	Fair.
Eurydice	Greek	The goddess of the underworld in Greek mythology.
Eustacia	Greek	Fruitful. The feminine form of Eustace.
Eva		Life-giving. Also see Evelyn.
Evadine	Greek	From Greek mythology.
Evadne	Greek	Fortunate.
Evana	East European	God is gracious. .
Evangelia	Greek	One who brings good news.
Evangeline	Greek	The bearer of good news.
Evania	Greek	Peaceful, tranquil.
Evanthe	Greek	Flower.
Eve	Hebrew	Life-giving. Also see Evelyn.
Evelina	Hebrew	Life giving.
Evelyn	English	From an old surname, but also related to Eve.
Everild	Old English	The slayer of the boar.
Everilda		The slayer of the boar.
Evette		From the name Yvonne. The feminine form of Yves. The little archer.
Evie		Life-giving.
Evita	Spanish	Life-giving.
Evonne	French/Greek	French: An archer. Greek: The wood of the Yew tree.

Ewa	Polish	Life-giving. Also see Evelyn.
Eyota	Native American	The greatest.
Fabia	Latin	A bean grower. Feminine form of Fabian.
Fabiana	Latin	Bean grower.
Fabienne	French	Bean grower.
Fabiola	French	Bean grower.
Fabrianne	Latin	Resourceful, or a craftswoman.
Fadila	Arabic	Generous and distinguished.
Fae	English from Old French	A fairy or magical creature. Also a diminutive of Faith.
Faiga	Germanic	A bird.
Faina	Anglo-Saxon	Joyful.
Fainche	Celtic	A saint's name.
Faine	Old English	Joyful.
Fairlee	Old English	
Fairley	Old English	A clearing in the woods.
Fairuza	Turkish	Turquoise.
Faith	English	Trusting in God, having faith. Also see Fidela.
Faiza	Arabic	Victorious.
Faizah	African	Victorious.
Fala	Native American	Crow.
Falda	Icelandic	With folded wings.
Falguni	Hindu	
Fallon	Irish	A leader.
Fanchon	French	From France, or a free woman. The feminine form of Francis.
Fannie		From France, or a free woman. The feminine form of Francis.
Fanny		From France, or a free woman. The feminine form of Francis.
Fantasia	Latin	Asia, Fanta
Fantine	French	Childlike.
Farah	Arabic	Happiness.
Farfalla	Italian	Butterfly.
Farica		A peaceful ruler. The feminine form of Frederick.
Farida	Arabic	Unique.
Fariishta	Urdu	Angel.

Farika		A peaceful ruler. The feminine form of Frederick.
Farley	Old English	From the fern clearing.
Farrah	Old English	Beautiful.
Fascienne	Latin	Black.
Fatima	Arabic	A woman who abstains, or weans a child. Also - a daughter of the prophet Mohamed.
Fatin	Arabic	Captivating.
Faustine	Latin	The fortunate one.
Fawn	Old French	A young deer.
Fawne	Old French, Latin	A young deer.
Fay	English from Old French	A fairy or magical creature. Also a diminutive of Faith.
Faye	Old French	Fairy or elf.
Fayina	Russian	Free one.
Faylinn		Fairy kingdom.
Fayme	Latin	Of high reputation, renowned.
Fayna		Joyful.
Fayne		Joyful.
Fayre	Old English	Fair.
Felcia	Polish	Lucky.
Felda	Teutonic	From the field.
Felice	Italian	Fortunate, happy.
Felicia		Happiness.
Felicite	French	Fortunate.
Felicity	Latin	Lucky, fortunate. The feminine form of Felix.
Felipa	Spanish	A lover of horses. The feminine form of Philip.
Femi	African	Love me.
Fenella	Irish	The white or fair shouldered one.
Fennella	Irish	The white or fair shouldered one.
Feodora	Russian	The gift of God. The feminine form of Theodore. Also see Dorothy.
Fern	Old English	Fern-like. From the plant name.
Fernanda	Teutonic	Prepared for the journey. A traveler or adventurer. The feminine form of Ferdinand.
Feronia	Latin	A mythological goddess.
Fidela	Latin	Faithful. Also see Faith.

Fidelia	Spanish	Faithful.
Fidelima	Irish Gaelic	The name of a saint.
Fifi		God shall add. The feminine form of Joseph.
Filberta		Very brilliant.
Filbertha		Very brilliant.
Filipina	Polish	Lover of horses.
Filippa	Italian	A lover of horses. The feminine form of Philip.
Filomena		A lover of the moon.
Filomene		A lover of the moon.
Findabhair	Gaelic	Finn.
Finola		The white or fair shouldered one.
Finvarra	Gaelic	
Fiona	Scottish Gaelic/Irish Gaelic	Scottish Gaelic: The fair one. Irish Gaelic: A vine.
Fionavar	Gaelic	
Fionn	Celtic	White, fair.
Fionola		The white or fair shouldered one.
Fiorella	Italian	A little flower.
Fiorenza	Italian	Flower.
Firaki	Hindu	
Flanna	Gaelic	Red-haired.
Flavia	Latin	The golden-haired one.
Fleta	Old English	Swift, fleet.
Fleur	Old French	A flower. Also see Flora.
Flo		Blossoming, flourishing.
Flora	Latin	A flower. After the Roman goddess of flowers and the spring. Also see Fleur.
Floramaria		Flower of Mary.
Florence	Latin	Blossoming, flourishing.
Floria		Flowering.
Floriane		Flowering.
Florizel		From Shakespeare's play Winter's Tale.
Flos	Norse	Chieftain.
Flower		Blossoming, flourishing.
Floy	Old German	
Fola	African	Honor.
Fonda	Latin	Affectionate.

Name	Origin	Meaning
Fortuna	Latin	The fortunate one.
Fosetta	French	The dimpled one.
Fotini	Greek	Light.
Fran		From France, or a free woman. The feminine form of Francis.
Frances	Latin	From France, or a free woman. The feminine form of Francis.
Francisca	Spanish	From France, or a free woman. The feminine form of Francis.
Freda		A wise counselor From the name Alfreda, Frederica, Winifred.
Frederica	Teutonic	A peaceful ruler. The feminine form of Frederick.
Frederika	Old German	Peaceful ruler.
Fredrica		Peace.
Freya		A lady. The goddess of love in Scandinavian mythology.
Freyde	Yiddish	Joy.
Frida		A wise counselor. From the name Alfreda, Frederica, Winifred.
Frieda		A wise counselor. From the name Alfreda, Frederica, Winifred.
Fritzi	German	A peaceful ruler. The feminine form of Frederick.
Fronde	Latin	A leaf of the fens.
Fruma	Yiddish	One who is religious.
Fuensanta	Spanish	A holy fountain.
Fujita	Japanese	Field.
Fulvia	Latin	Tawny haired. The name of the wife of Mark Antony.
Fuscienne	Latin	Black.
Gabby		God is my strength.
Gabi		God is my strength.
Gabriel	Hebrew	God is my strength. One of the archangels in the Bible.
Gabriela		God is my strength.
Gabriella		God is my strength.
Gabrielle		God is my strength.
Gaby		God is my strength.
Gadar	Armenian	Perfection.
Gae		Blithe, cheerful.

Gaea	Greek	Goddess of the Earth
Gai		Blithe, cheerful.
Gaia	Greek	The Earth. The Earth goddess in Greek mythology.
Gail	Hebrew	Father's joy. A short form of Abigail.
Gainell	unknown	To profit.
Gaines	Middle English	Increase in wealth, to grow rich.
Gajendra	Hindu	Elephant king.
Gala	Swedish	Singer.
Galatea	Greek	Milky white. A figure from Greek mythology.
Gale		A stranger.
Galen	Greek	The calm one, or the helper.
Galena	Latin	A lead-like metal.
Gali	Hebrew	Spring, fountain.
Galia	Hebrew	A wave.
Galiena	Teutonic	A lofty maiden.
Galina	Russian from Greek	Calm. Also see Helen.
Galya	Hebrew	God has redeemed.
Gana	Hebrew	A garden.
Ganesa	Hindu	Good luck.
Gardenia		A flower name.
Gargi	Hindu	
Garland	Old French	A crown or wreath of flowers.
Garnet	Old French	Dark red, from the color of pomegranates. Also the name of a gemstone.
Gauri	Hindu	Yellow.
Gavrila	Hebrew	A heroine.
Gay	Old French	Blithe, cheerful.
Gayatri	Hindu	Mother of the Vedas.
Gaye		Merry, happy.
Gayle	Hebrew	Father's joy.
Gayleen	Hebrew	Father's joy.
Gaylene	Hebrew	Father's joy.
Gaynor	Welsh	Fair and soft.
Gazelle	Latin	The antelope.
Gebriele	Hebrew	A woman of God. The feminine form of Gabriel.
Gedala	Aboriginal	The day.

Gelasia	Greek	Laughing, like a bubbling spring.
Gelsey	Persian	A flower.
Gemina	Greek	A twin.
Gemma	Italian	A jewel or gem.
Gena		Noble, well-born.
Gene	Greek	Noble, well-born.
Genesia	Latin	The newcomer.
Genesis	Hebrew	Origin.
Genette		God is gracious. The feminine form of John.
Geneva		After the city in Switzerland. Also see Genevieve.
Genevieve	Old French	A woman of the people.
Genie		Noble, well-born.
Genista	Latin	From the name of the broom plant.
Genji	Chinese	Gold.
Genna		Fair and soft.
Gennifer		Fair and soft.
Genny		Fair and soft.
Georgette		A girl from the farm. The feminine form of George.
Georgia		A girl from the farm.
Georgina	Greek	A girl from the farm.
Geraldine	English from Old French	A noble spear-carrier. The feminine form of Gerald.
Geranium	Greek	A flower name.
Gerarda	English from Old French	A brave spear woman. The feminine form of Gerard. Also see Geraldine.
Gerda	Old Norse	Protected one.
Gerlinde	Teutonic	Of the weak spear.
Germaine	French	From Germany.
Gerry	English from Old French	A spear warrior.
Gertrude	Teutonic	A spear maiden.
Geva	Hebrew	Hill.
Ghada	Arabic	Graceful.
Ghera	Aboriginal	A gum leaf.
Ghislain		A pledge.
Ghislaine	French	A pledge.
Ghita	Italian	Pearl.
Giacinta	Italian	Young and beautiful.

Gianina	Italian	God is gracious.
Gianna	Italian	God is gracious.
Gigi	French	A girl from the farm. The feminine form of George.
Gil		Short for names beginning with Gil.
Gilana	Hebrew	Joy.
Gilberta	Teutonic	A bright or famous pledge. The feminine form of Gilbert.
Gilda	Teutonic	A sacrifice.
Gilen	Teutonic	Industrious pledge.
Gili		My joy, rejoice.
Gillian	Latin	From a Roman family name. The feminine form of Julian and a derivative of Julia.
Gin	Japanese	Silver.
Gina	Greek	A girl from the farm. From Georgina. The feminine form of George.
Ginette		A woman of the people.
Ginevra	Italian	A woman of the people.
Ginger		Maidenly, pure. Also name of a spice.
Ginny		Maidenly, pure. From the name Virginia.
Giorgetta	Italian	A girl from the farm. The feminine form of George.
Giorgia		A girl from the farm. The feminine form of George.
Giorgio		A girl from the farm. The feminine form of George.
Giovanna	Italian	God is gracious.
Girija	Hindu	
Gisela	Dutch/Greman	A pledge.
Giselle	Teutonic	A pledge.
Gita	Sanskrit	A song.
Gitana	Spanish	The gipsy.
Gitanjali	Hindu	
Githa	Anglo-Saxon	Gift.
Gitika	Hindu	
Giulia	Italian	From a Roman, possibly meaning youthful.
Giulietta	Italian	From a Roman, possibly meaning youthful.

Giuseppina	Italian	God shall add.
Gizane	Basque	Christ's incarnation.
Gladys	Welsh	The lame one.
Gleda	Old English	To make happy.
Glen	Gaelic/Welsh/Cornish	From the valley or glen.
Glenda	Welsh	Pure and good.
Glenna	Gaelic	From the valley.
Glennis	Gaelic	From the valley or glen.
Glenys	Welsh	Holy, pure.
Glora		Glorious.
Gloria	Latin	Glorious.
Glynis	Latin	Holy, pure.
Glynnis	Latin	Holy, pure.
Godiva	Old English	The gift of God.
Goldie	English	The golden one. Also a form of the Yiddish name Golda.
Goneril		From Shakespeare's play King Lear.
Gordana	Serbian	Proud. Feminine form of Gordon.
Gotzone	Basque	Angel, messenger.
Grace	Latin	Graceful.
Gracie		Graceful.
Graeae	Greek	Gray ones
Grania	Irish Gaelic	The name of a figure in Irish legend.
Grear	Scottish	Watchful.
Greer	Scottish	Watchful, vigilant.
Gregoria	Greek	Watchful, vigilant.
Greta	German/Swedish	A pearl.
Gretchen	German	A pearl.
Grete		A pearl.
Gretel	Swiss	A pearl.
Grette	Danish	A pearl.
Grier	Scottish	Watchful, vigilant.
Griselda	Teutonic	The grey battle heroine.
Gryffyn	Comish/Welsh	Mythological winged beast.
Guadalupe	Arabic	The river of the wolf. Generally a Spanish name.
Guan-yin	Chinese	The goddess of mercy.
Guda	Old English	Good.
Guddu	Hindu	

Gudrun	Old Norse	Divine lore or wisdom.
Guenevere		Fair one.
Guida	Latin	The guide.
Guinevere	Welsh	Fair and soft. Wife of legendary King Arthur.
Gulara	Aboriginal	Moonlight.
Gunda		Female warrior.
Gunnhild	Old Norse	A maiden of battle.
Gurley	Aboriginal	A native willow.
Guyra	Aboriginal	A fishing place, or a white cockatoos. Also a location.
Gwen	Welsh	Fair, or blessed.
Gwendolen	Welsh	A white ring or bow.
Gwendolyn		Goddess of the moon.
Gwenhyvar	Welsh	Gwen
Gwennap	Cornish	The name of a saint and a location.
Gwyn	Welsh	White, fair, or blessed.
Gwyneth	Welsh	From a region of North Wales.
Gylay	Turkish	Rose, moon.
Gymea	Aboriginal	A small bird.
Gypsy	Old English	A wanderer.
Gytha	Old English	Warlike.
Ha-Neul	Korean	Sky.
Habiba	Arabic	The beloved, the dew one.
Habika	African	Sweetheart.
Hadara	Hebrew	Overly beautiful.
Hadassa	Hebrew	Flowering myrtle.
Hadassah	Jewish	A star.
Hadil	Arabic	Cooing like a dove.
Hadiya	Arabic/Swahili	A gift.
Hadria	Italian	A dark woman from the sea.
Hadya	Arabic	A leader or guide.
Hafwen	Welsh	As beautiful as summer.
Hagar	Hebrew	Forsaken, or taking flight.
Haidce	Greek	Modest.
Haifa	Arabic	Slender.
Haimi	Hawaiian	The seeker.
Haja		
Hala	Arabic	A halo around the moon.
Halcyone	Greek	The kingfisher.

Haldana	Old Norse	Half Danish.
Haldis	Teutonic, Norse	Stone spirit, reliable, assistant.
Haleigha	Hawaiian	House of the rising sun.
Haley	Irish Gaelic	Ingenious.
Halfrida	Teutonic	A peaceful heroine.
Hali	Greek, Hebrew	Sea, necklace, a location.
Halia	Greek	The sun.
Haliey		A high clearing or meadow.
Halima	African	Gentle.
Hallie	Greek	Thinking of the sea.
Halona	Native American	Fortunate.
Hana	Arabic	Bliss, happiness.
Hanan	Hebrew	Arabic: The affectionate one. Hebrew: The gracious gift of God.
Hanna		Goddess of life.
Hannah	Hebrew	Favored by God, or graceful.
Hanne		God is gracious.
Hansine	German from Hebrew	God is gracious. A feminine form of Ham.
Hanya	Aboriginal	A stone.
Happy	English	Bright and cheerful.
Haralda	Old English	The ruler of the army. Feminine form of Harold.
Harika	Turkish	Wonderful.
Harley	Old English	From the hare or stag meadow.
Harmony	Greek	Concordant, in harmony.
Harper	Old English	A harp player or maker.
Harriet	Teutonic	The ruler of the home. A feminine form of Harry.
Harsha	Hindu	
Harshita	Hindu	
Haruko	Japanese	Spring.
Harva		Army warrior. Feminine form of Harvey.
Hasina	Swahili	Good.
Hasna	Arabic	Beautiful.
Hathor	Egyptian	The goddess of love and joy.
Hattie		The ruler of the home.
Hava	Jewish	Life-giving.
Havana	Spanish	The capital of Cuba.

Haya	Hebrew	Life.
Hayfa	Arabic	Slender, delicate.
Haylee	Old English	From the hay meadow.
Hayley	Old English	A high clearing or meadow.
Hazel	Old English	From the Hazel tree.
Hazelle		From the Hazel tree.
Hea	Korean	Grace.
Heater		A star.
Heather	Old English	A flower name.
Heba	Hebrew	Gift from God.
Hebe	Greek	Youthful. A goddess of youth in mythology.
Hedasaa	Jewish	A star.
Hedda	Scandinavian	The contentious one. A fighter.
Hedea	Greek	Pleasing.
Hedia	Hebrew	Voice of the Lord.
Hedva	Hebrew	Joy.
Hedwig	Teutonic	The contentious one. A fighter.
Hedy		The contentious one. A fighter.
Heidi	Swiss	Noble and kind.
Heledd	Welsh	A traditional name.
Helen	Greek	The light of the sun.
Helena		The light of the sun.
Helene	French	The light of the sun.
Helga	Old Norse	Successful, prosperous. Also see Olga.
Heli	Finish	Sun.
Helice	Greek	A spiel.
Helima	Arabic	Kind, gentle.
Helina	Russian	The light of the sun.
Helki	Miwok Indian	To touch.
Helma	German	The resolute protector.
Helmine	German	The resolute protector.
Heloise		Agreeable.
Helouse		Healthy.
Helvetia	Latin	A woman from Switzerland.
Hem	Hindu	
Hema	Hindu	Snow, Himalayas.
Hemangi	Hindu	
Hemangini	Hindu	

Hemlata	Hindu	
Heng	Chinese	
Henka	Teutonic	Ruler of an estate.
Henrietta	Teutonic	The ruler of the home.
Hera	Latin from Greek	A queen. The wife of Zeus, ruler of the heavens, in Greek mythology.
Hermelinda	Spanish	Shield of power.
Hermia		From Shakespeare's play Midsummer-Night's Dream.
Herminia	Spanish	Lady of the Earth.
Hermione	Greek	A handsome figure in Greek mythology. The feminine form of Achilles.
Hermosa	Spanish	Beautiful.
Hero		From Shakespeare's play Much Ado About Nothing.
Herschell	unknown	Deer.
Herta		Of the earth.
Hertha		Of the earth.
Hesper	Greek	The evening star. Also see Esther.
Hester		Star.
Hestia	Greek	The goddess of the hearth.
Hetal	Hindu	
Hettie		The ruler of the home. A feminine form of Harry.
Hetty		The ruler of the home. A feminine form of Harry.
Hibernia	Latin	A woman from Ireland.
Hibiscus	Greek	A flower name.
Hide	Japanese	Excellent, fruitful.
Hidi	African	Root.
Hika	Polynesian	A daughter.
Hilary	Latin	The cheerful one.
Hilda	Teutonic	A battle maiden.
Hilde		A battle maiden.
Hildegard	Teutonic	A battle stronghold.
Hildemar	Teutonic	Decorated in battle.
Hillary		The cheerful one.
Hilzarie		Moon and stars.
Hina	Hindu	

Hinda	Jewish	A female deer.
Hine	Polynesian	A maiden.
Hippolyta	Greek	She who frees the horses. Also from Shakespeare's play Midsummer-Night's Dream.
Hiriwa	Polynesian	Silver.
Hiroko	Japanese	Generous.
Hisa	Japanese	Long-lasting.
Hjordis	Old Norse	A sword goddess.
Hoku	Polynesian	A star.
Holda	Teutonic	Concealed.
Holli	Teutonic	From the name Holly.
Holly	Old English	From the name of the tree. Suitable for a child born around Christmas.
Honey	Old English	The sweet one.
Honna	Greek	
Honora	Latin	Honor.
Honour	Latin	Honorable.
Hope	Old English	Hopeful, optimistic.
Horatia	Latin	From a Roman family name. The feminine form of Horace.
Hortense	Latin	The garden lover.
Hoshi	Japanese	A star.
Hua	Chinese	A flower.
Huberta	Teutonic	A brilliant mind. The feminine form of the boy's name of Hubert.
Hue	Vietnamese	Lily.
Huette	French from Teutonic	Heart and mind.
Hulda	Hebrew/Old Norse	Hebrew: A weasel. Old Norse: Lovable.
Huon		The name of a Tasmanian river and a type of tree.
Huyana	Native American	Raining.
Hyacinth	Greek	Young and beautiful. Also a flower name.
Hye	unknown	Gracefulness.
Hylda		A battle maiden.
Hypatia	Greek	The highest.
Ianna		God is gracious. Feminine form of Ian.
Ianthe	Greek	A violet-colored flower.

Ida	Teutonic	Happy, or youthful.
Ideh	Hebrew	Praise.
Idelia	Teutonic	Noble.
Idola	Greek	Idolized.
Idona	Old Norse	After the name of a Norse goddess who was in charge of the apples of eternal youth.
Idonia	Old German	Industrious.
Idra	Aramaic	A fig tree.
Idylla	Greek	Perfect.
Ierne	Latin	From Ireland.
Ignatia	Latin	Ardent, fiery. Feminine form of Ignatius.
Iku	Japanese	Nourishing.
Ila	Old French	From the island.
Ilana	Hebrew	Great tree.
Ilanna	Hebrew	A tree.
Ilaria	Latin	One who is merry, joyful.
Ildiko	Hungarian	A fierce warrior.
Ileana	Greek	From the city of (Lion). Also a Romanian form of Helen.
Ilena	Irish	The light of the sun. The Irish form of Helen.
Ilene	Irish	The light of the sun. The Irish form of Helen.
Ilisapesi	Tonga	Blessed one.
Ilka		The light of the sun.
Illona	Irish	The light of the sun.
Ilona		Hungarian form of Helen.
Ilsa		Consecrated to God.
Ilse	German	Short form of Elizabeth, meaning consecrated to God.
Iluka	Aboriginal	Near the sea.
Ima	Japanese	Now, the present.
Imam	Arabic	One who believes in God.
Iman	Arabic	Faith, belief.
Imelda	Italian/Spanish	A floret.
Immacolata	Italian	The immaculate conception of Christ.
Imogen	Celtic/Latin	Celtic: A girl or maiden. Latin: The image of her mother.

Imogen	Celtic/Latin	Celtic: A girl or maiden. Latin: The image of her mother.
Imogene	Latin	Image.
Imperia	Latin	Imperious, the imperial one.
Ina		Pure, chaste.
Inari	Finnish	A lake.
Inas	Polynesian	The wife of the moon.
Inayat	Hindu	Kindness.
Indaliai	Hindu	Seafarer.
India		From the name of the country. Also a character in the novel and film, Gone with the Wind.
Indira	Sanskrit	An alternative name for Lakshmi, wife of the god Vishnu.
Indrina	Hindu	Deep.
Indu	Hindu	
Ines		Pure, chaste.
Inez		Pure, chaste.
Inga	Old Norse	Hero's daughter.
Ingaberg	Old Norse	Hero's daughter.
Ingaborg	Old Norse	Hero's daughter.
Inge	Old Norse	Hero's daughter.
Inger	Old Norse	A son's army or a Hero's daughter.
Ingrid	Old Norse	Hero's daughter.
Iniga		Ardent, fiery. Feminine form of Ignatius.
Innocentia	Latin	Innocent.
Io	Greek	
Iola	Greek	Violet-colored
Iolana	Hawaiian	To soar like an eagle.
Iolanthe	Greek	A violet flower. The title of a Gilbert and Sullivan opera.
Iona	Scottish/Aboriginal	Scottish: The name of a Hebridean island. Aboriginal: A tree.
Ione	Greek	A violet-colored stone.
Iphigenia	Greek	The daughter of Agamemnon in Greek mythology.
Iratze	Basque	In reference to the Virgin Mary.
Irene	Greek	Peace.
Ireta	Latin	Angry enraged.

Irihapeti	Maori	A form of Elizabeth, meaning consecrated to God.
Irina	East European	Peace.
Iris	Greek	A rainbow and a flower.
Irma	Latin/Teutonic	Latin: Noble. Teutonic: Whole, strong.
Irmgard		
Irvette	Old English	A friend from the sea.
Isa	Sanskrit/Teutonic	Sanskrit: A lord. Teutonic: Strong-willed.
Isabel	Spanish	A form of Elizabeth, meaning consecrated to God.
Isabella	Italian	A form of Elizabeth, meaning consecrated to God.
Isadora	Greek	The gift of Isis. Feminine form of Isidore.
Isaura	Greek	Soft air.
Iseult		The fair one.
Ishana	Hindu	Rich.
Ishi	Japanese	A stone.
Ishita	Hindu	
Isis	Egyptian	After the goddess of fertility. The supreme goddess.
Isla	Scottish	From the name of an island.
Isleen		The light of the sun. The Irish form of Helen.
Isleta	Spanish	Little Island.
Ismena	Greek	Learned.
Isobel		A form of Elizabeth, meaning consecrated to God.
Isoke	African	Satisfying gift.
Isola	Latin	Isolated. A loner.
Isolde	Welsh	The fair one.
Isra	Arabic	Journeying by night.
Israt	Arabic	Affection.
Istas	Native American	Snow.
Ita	Irish Gaelic	Thirsty.
Iti	Hindu	
Itzel	Mayan	
Iva	Old French	A Yew tree.
Ivana	Czech	God is gracious.
Ivanna	Russian	God is gracious.
Ivory	Latin	From the tusks of an elephant.

Ivy	Old English	Plant name.
Ixchel	Majan	Goddess of the moon and fertility
Izanami	Japanese	She who invites you to enter.
Jacinda	Greek	Beautiful.
Jacinta	Spanish from Greek	Beautiful. Also a form of Hyacinth.
Jacinthe	Greek	hyacinth
Jacki		The supplanter. The feminine form of Jacob and James.
Jackie		The supplanter.
Jacky		The supplanter.
Jaclyn		The supplanter.
Jacoba	Hebrew	The supplanter.
Jacqueline	French from Hebrew	The supplanter.
Jacqui		The supplanter.
Jada	Hebrew	Wise.
Jade	Spanish	The jade stone.
Jadwiga	Polish	The contentious one. A fighter.
Jael	Hebrew	To ascend or a wild goat.
Jaen	Hebrew	Ostrich.
Jaffa	Hebrew	Beautiful.
Jagrati	Hindu	
Jahnavi	Hindu	
Jaime	French	French for I love you.
Jaimica	Spanish	Supplanter.
Jaimie	French	I love.
Jaina	Hindu	Good character.
Jaione	Basque	Nativity.
Jakinda	Basque	Hyacinth.
Jala	Arabic	Charity.
Jamal	Arabic	The handsome one.
Jamari	French	Warrior.
Jamee	Hebrew	Supplanter, one who replaces.
Jamesina	Hebrew	The supplanter.
Jamila	Arabic/Swahili	Beautiful.
Jamilah	Arabic	Beautiful.
Jan		God is gracious.
Jana		God is gracious.

Jancis	English	A modern name derived from Jane and Frances. Jane - God is gracious. Frances - From France, or a free woman.
Jane	Hebrew	God is gracious. The feminine form of John.
Janelle	English	A modern name derived from Jane and the feminine suffix `elle'. Jane - God is gracious.
Janet		God is gracious. The feminine form of John.
Janette		God is gracious.
Janice		God is gracious.
Janina		God is gracious.
Janine		God is gracious.
Janisa		Funny, loveable, hyper child.
Janna	Hebrew	Flourishing.
Jannali	Aboriginal	The moon. Also a location.
Janthina		A violet-colored flower.
Janthine		A violet-colored flower.
Japera		
Jaquenetta	French from Hebrew	The supplanter.
Jarah	Hebrew	Honey.
Jardena	Hebrew	To flow downward.
Jarita	Sanskrit	A legendary bird.
Jarka	Slavonic	Springlike.
Jarmila	Slavonic	The grace of spring.
Jarrah	Aboriginal	A type of Eucalyptus tree.
Jarvia	Teutonic	As sharp or keen as a spear.
Jarvinia	German	Keen intelligence.
Jasmine	Persian	A fragrant flower.
Jaunie		
Jaya	Sanskrit	Victory. Also the name of a Buddhist female goddess.
Jayani	Hindu	A Sakti of Ganesha.
Jayne	Hindu	Victorious.
Jaythen	Swedish	
Jazlyn	Arabic	
Jean	French	God is gracious.
Jeanne	French	God is gracious.
Jeannette		God is gracious.
Jehan	Arabic	Beautiful flower.

Jelena	Russian	shining light
Jemima	Hebrew	A dove. A biblical name.
Jemma		A jewel or gem.
Jena		God is gracious.
Jenara		
Jenay	French	Name of a plant.
Jendayi	African	Give thanks.
Jendyose	Ugandan	Have done good to produce a child.
Jenell	German	Knowledge, understanding, kindness.
Jenica	Romanian	God is gracious
Jenna		Fair and soft.
Jennifer	Cornish/Welsh	Fair and soft. Also a variation of Guinevere.
Jenny		Fair and soft.
Jeno	Greek	Heaven, well-born.
Jensine	Hebrew	God is gracious
Jeraldine		A noble spear-carrier.
Jerarda		A brave spear woman. The feminine form of Gerard.
Jeremia	Hebrew	Appointed by God. The feminine form of Jeremiah and Jeremy.
Jermain		From Germany.
Jermayne		From Germany.
Jerrica		
Jerusha	Hebrew	The married one.
Jesal	Hindu	
Jess		Wealthy.
Jesse	Hebrew	God's gift.
Jessica	Hebrew	Wealthy. Used by Shakespeare for a character in The Merchant of Venice.
Jessie		Wealthy. Also independent names, particularly in Scotland.
Jet	Latin	Black, the name of a material used for making jewelery
Jetta	Latin	Black, the name of a material used for making jewelery
Jewel	Old French	A gemstone or the precious one.
Jewell		A gemstone or the precious one.
Jezebel		Impure.

Jezreel	Hebrew	
Jiba	Aboriginal	The moon.
Jiera	Lithuanian	Living.
Jigisha	Hindu	
Jihan	Turkish	Universe.
Jill		From a Roman family name. The feminine form of Julian and a derivative of Julia.
Jilli		From a Roman family name.
Jillian		From a Roman family name.
Jillie		From a Roman family name.
Jilly		From a Roman family name.
Jin	Chinese/Korean	Chinese: Golden. Korean: A jewel.
Jina	Swahili	Name.
Jinx	Latin	A charm.
Jirra	Aboriginal	A kangaroo.
Joakima	Hebrew	The Lord will judge.
Joan		God is gracious.
Joann		God is gracious.
Joanna		God is gracious.
Joanne		God is gracious.
Jobey	Hebrew	Persecuted.
Jobina	Hebrew	The persecuted one. The female form of Job. Biblical origin.
Jocasta	Greek	The shining moon. The mother of Oedipus in Greek mythology.
Jocelyn	Latin	The merry one.
Jocosa	Latin	Humorous, playful.
Jocunda	Latin	Cheerful, merry.
Jodi		God is gracious.
Jodie		A woman from Judea.
Joelle	French from Hebrew	The Lord is God. The feminine form of Joel.
Joelliane	Hebrew	Jehova is God.
Joesa		
Johanna		God is gracious.
Jolan	Hungarian	Violet blossom.
Jolanda	Italian	A violet flower.
Jolanta	Polish	A violet flower.

Jolene	English	A modern combination, perhaps of Jo and Marlene.
Jolie	French	Pretty.
Jonesy	Old English	
Joni		God is gracious.
Jonie		God is gracious.
Jonina	Hebrew	Dove.
Jonquil		A flower name, from the Latin word for a reed.
Joo-Eun	Korean	Silver pearl.
Jora	Hebrew	autumn rain
Jordan	Hebrew	Flowing down, as in the River Jordan.
Jordana	Hebrew	Flowing down, as in the River Jordan.
Jordane	Hebrew	Descendant, flowing down.
Joscelin		The merry one.
Josephine	Hebrew	God shall add. The feminine form of Joseph.
Josie		God will add.
Joslin		The merry one.
Josslyn		The merry one.
Jovita		The joyful one.
Joy	Latin	Joyful.
Joyanne	Latin	A combination of joy and Anne.
Joyce	Middle English	A lord. Originally a boys name.
Juana	Spanish	God is gracious.
Juanita	Spanish	God is gracious.
Judith	Hebrew	A woman from Judea. A name from the Bible.
Judy		A woman from Judea.
Juene	French	Young.
Juhi	Hindu	
Jules		Youthful.
Julia	Latin	From a Roman, possibly meaning youthful.
Juliana		Soft-haired.
Julianna		From the name Julia & Anne.
Julianne		From the name Julia & Anne.
Julie	French	From a Roman, possibly meaning youthful.
Juliet		From a Roman name, possibly meaning youthful.

Julinka	Latin	Youthful.
Julya	Russian	From a Roman, possibly meaning youthful.
Jumoke	Nigerian	The beloved one.
Jun	Chinese	The truth.
June	English	From the month of June.
Juniper	Latin	From the name of die juniper plant.
Juno	Latin	The heavenly one. The wife of Jupiter in Roman mythology. Also a form of Una.
Justine	Latin	Fair, just. The feminine form of Justin.
Jutta		A woman from Judea, praised one.
Jutte		A woman from Judea, praised one.
Jyoti	Sanskrit	Light.
Jyotsna	Hindu	
Kaatje	Dutch	Pure.
Kachine	Native American	Sacred dancer.
Kade	Indonesian	A popular girl's name.
Kadee	Aboriginal	Mother.
Kadija	African	The prophet's wife.
Kadira	Arabic	Powerful.
Kadisha	Hebrew	Holy.
Kaede	Japanese	Maple leaf.
Kaelyn	Old English	Meadow.
Kaer	Breton	Form of Katherine.
Kaethe	Greek	Pure.
Kagami	Japanese	A motor.
Kai	Hawaiian, Navajo Indian	Sea, willow tree.
Kaia	Greek	Earth.
Kaie	Celtic	Combat.
Kaili	Hawaiian	A deity.
Kaimi	Polynesian	The seeker.
Kairos	Greek	Goddess from Jupiter.
Kaitlyn		Pure.
Kaiya	Aboriginal	A type of spear.
Kaja		A daisy.
Kajal	Hindu	Eyeliner.
Kajol	Hindu	

Kajsa	Swedish	
Kakra	Ghanese	Younger of twins.
Kala	Aboriginal	Fire.
Kalama	Hawaiian	Flaming torch.
Kalanit	Hebrew	Flower name.
Kalantha		A beautiful blossom.
Kalare	Latin	Bright, clear.
Kalea	Hawaiian	Bright.
Kaley		A warrior maid.
Kali	Sanskrit	Black.
Kalie	Dutch	Kali
Kalika	Greek	A rosebud.
Kalila	Arabic	Beloved.
Kalinda	Sanskrit/Aboriginal	Sanskrit: The sea. Aboriginal: A lookout.
Kaliska	Miwok Indian	Coyote chasing deer.
Kalista		The most beautiful one.
Kalle	Finnish	Strong.
Kalliope		A beautiful voice. The muse of poetry in Greek mythology.
Kalonice	Greek	Beauty's victory.
Kalpana	Sanskrit	A fantasy.
Kalyani	Sanskrit	Auspicious, beautiful.
Kalypso		A legendary sea nymph. Also a West Indian style of music.
Kama	Sanskrit/Thai	Sanskrit: The golden one. Thai: Love.
Kamakshi	Hindu	A Devi, same as Lalita.
Kamala	Sanskrit	A loin.
Kamali	Rhodesian	Spirit protector.
Kamaria	Swahili	Like the moon.
Kamballa	Aboriginal	A young woman.
Kambo	African	Must work for everything.
Kamea	Hawaiian	
Kameko	Japanese	The child of the tortoise.
Kamil	Arabic/Czech	Arabic: Perfect. Czech: From a Roman family name.
Kamila	Czech/Polish	From a Roman family name, possibly meaning noble.
Kamilah	Arabic	The perfect one.
Kamilia	Polish	Ceremonial attendant.

Kamna	Hindu	Desire.
Kamryn	Kami, Kam	
Kanchana	Hindu	A celestial Apsara, gold.
Kane	Irish Gaelic	Warlike.
Kanene	African	A little thing in the eye is big.
Kanika	Kenyan	Black cloth.
Kaniya	Native American	
Kantha	Hindu	Name of a God.
Kanti	Sanskrit	Lovely.
Kanushi	Hindu	
Kanya	Thai	A young lady.
Kapera	African	This child, too, will die.
Kara		Irish Gaelic: A friend. Cornish: Love. Italian: The beloved one.
Karel	Czech/Dutch	A free person.
Karen		Pure, virginal.
Karena		Pure one.
Karensa		Love.
Karenza		Love.
Karida	Arabic	Untouched, virginal.
Karima	Arabic	Noble, generous.
Karimah	African	Generous.
Karishma	Hindu	
Karissa	Greek	Love, grace.
Karita	Scandinavian	Loving and benevolent. .
Karka	Hindu	Crab.
Karla		A free person.
Karli		Little and womanly.
Karlotte		A free person.
Karly		A free person.
Karma	Tibetan/Sherpa	A star.
Karmel		A garden or orchard.
Karmina		Song, songstress.
Karol	Polish	A free person.
Karolina		A free person.
Karoline		A free person.
Karri	Aboriginal	A type of Eucalyptus.
Karuah	Aboriginal	A native Plum tree.
Karyan	Armenian	The dark one.
Kasa	Hopi Indian	Fur-robe dress.

Kasinda	African	Born to a family with twins.
Kasmira	Old Slavic	Demands peace.
Katarina	Swedish	Pure.
Kate	Czech/Russian	Pure.
Katelin		Pure, virginal.
Katerina	Czech/Russian	Pure.
Katerine	Czech/Russian	Pure.
Katharina	Greek	Pure. The name of a 4th-century saint who was martyred on a wheel.
Katharine		Pure, virginal.
Katherine	Greek	Pure. The name of a 4th-century saint who was martyred on a wheel.
Kathie		Pure, virginal.
Kathleen	Irish	Pure, virginal.
Kathryn		Pure, virginal.
Kathy		From the name Katherine.
Katie		Pure, virginal.
Katina		Pure, unsullied.
Katren		Pure.
Katrin		Pure.
Katrina		Pure.
Katrine	German/Scandinavian	Pure.
Katy		Pure, virginal.
Katya		Pure, virginal.
Katyayani	Hindu	
Katyin	Aboriginal	Water.
Kaula	Polynesian	Prophet.
Kaveri	Hindu	Sacred river of India.
Kavindra	Hindu	Mighty poet.
Kavita	Hindu	Poem.
Kay	Welsh	Rejoiced in.
Kaya	Hopi Indian	My elder sister, little.
Kayla	Hebrew	Crown of laurels.
Kaylana		A combination of Kay and Lana.
Kaylee		A combination of Kay and Lana.
Kayley	Irish Gaelic	Slender.
Kayna	Cornish	A saint's name.
Kazanna		
Kazia	Hebrew	Plant with cinnamon-like bark.

Keandra	Hawaiian	
Keara	Irish	A saint's name.
Kebira	Arabic	Powerful.
Keeley	Irish Gaelic	Beautiful.
Keelin	Celtic	Slender, fair.
Keely	Gaelic	Beautiful and graceful.
Keera	Irish Gaelic	Dark, black. Feminine form of Kieran.
Kefira	Hebrew	Young lioness.
Kehinde	Yoruban	Second of twins.
Kei	Japanese	Rapture, reverence.
Keiko	Japanese	The beloved or adored one.
Keilana	Hawaiian	Adored one.
Keilantra	Hawaiian	Princess of the night sky, magical.
Keira	Irish Gaelic	Dark, black. Feminine form of Kieran.
Keisha	African	Favorite.
Kelda	Old Norse	A fountain or mountain spring.
Kelila	Hebrew	A crown of laurel.
Kellan	Gaelic	Warrior princess.
Kelley		Warrior or warrior woman.
Kelli		A warrior maid.
Kellsie		Island of the ships.
Kelly	Irish Gaelic	A warrior.
Kelsey	Old Norse	A dweller on the island or by the water.
Kendra	Celtic/Old English	Celtic: A hill. Old English: Royal power. Feminine form of Kendrick.
Kennis	Gaelic	Beautiful.
Kensington		
Kenwyn	Cornish/Welsh	The name of a saint.
Kenya		The name of an African country.
Kenyangi	Ugandan	White egret.
Kenyatta	Kenyan	
Kepa	Basque	Stone.
Kerani	Hindu	sacred bells
Keren	Hebrew	A ray, or a horn.
Kerensa	Cornish	Love.
Kerri		Dark and mysterious.

Kerry	Irish Gaelic	The dark one. Also the name of an Irish county.
Kerstin		Swedish form of Christina.
Kerzi	Turkish	
Kesare	Spanish	Long-haired.
Keshia	African	The favorite.
Kesi	Swahili	born when father was in trouble
Kesia	African	Favorite.
Kessie	Ghanese	Fat at birth.
Kestrel	English	From the bird name.
Ketaki	Hindu	
Ketika	Hindu	
Keturah	Hebrew	Fragrant incense.
Ketzia	Hebrew	Surface, cinnamon-like bark.
Keverne	Irish Gaelic	The name of a saint and a location.
Kevina		Handsome, beautiful.
Keyanna		Gracious.
Keyna	Welsh	A jewel.
Kezia	Hebrew	From the Cassia tree, a variety of cinnamon.
Khalida	Arabic	Eternal.
Khalidah	Arabic	Immortal.
Kiah	Aboriginal	From the beautiful place.
Kiana	Hawaiian	Moon Goddess.
Kiara		The name of an Irish saint.
Kichi	Japanese	Fortunate.
Kiden	African	Female born after 3 or more boys.
Kiele	Hawaiian	Gardenia, fragrant blossom.
Kiera	Irish Gaelic	Dark, black. Feminine form of Kieran.
Kiki	Egyptian	From the Castor plant.
Kiku	Japanese	A chrysanthemum.
Kiley		Good looking.
Kim	Vietnamese	The golden one or from the meadow..
Kimatra	Hindu	Seduce.
Kimba	Aboriginal	A bushfire.
Kimberley	Old English	From the meadow.
Kimberly		A diamond-filled rock.
Kineta	Greek	Active.

Kiona	Native American	Brown hills.
Kira	Persian	The sun.
Kirby	Teutonic/Old Norse	From the church village.
Kiri	Polynesian	The bark of a tree.
Kirilee		
Kirima	Eskimo	A hill.
Kirra	Aboriginal	A leaf.
Kirsten	Scandinavian	A follower of Christ, a Christian.
Kirstie	Scottish	A follower of Christ, a Christian.
Kirti	Hindu	Fame, a form of the Devi.
Kisa	Russian	Kitty, pure.
Kiska	Russian	Pure.
Kismet	Persian	Destiny.
Kissa	Ugandan	Born after twins.
Kit	Greek	Bearing Christ or pure.
Kita	Japanese	North.
Kitty	Greek	Pure. Also see Catherine, Karen and Kathleen.
Kitu	Hindu	
Kiyoko	Japanese	Clear.
Klara	German/Scandinavian	Bright and famous. The name of an Irish county.
Klarissa		The little brilliant one.
Klaudia	Polish	The lame one. The feminine form of Claude.
Klavdia	Slavic	A lame one.
Klea		
Klementyna	Polish	Mild, merciful.
Kleopatra		Glory of the father. The queen of Egypt from 47-30 BC.
Kohana	Japanese	A little flower.
Kohia	Polynesian	A passionflower.
Koko	Japanese/ Native American	Japanese: A stork. North American Indian: Of the night.
Kolina	Greek/Swedish	Greek: Pure. Swedish: A Maiden.
Kolora	Aboriginal	A freshwater lagoon.
Komal	Hindu	
Konstanze	German	Steadfast, constant.
Koorine	Aboriginal	A daughter.
Kora	Aboriginal	A companion.
Kordelia		A jewel of the sea.

Koren	Greek	A maiden.
Kornelia		A horn. The feminine form of Cornelius.
Korra	Aboriginal	Grass.
Kris	Greek	A follower of Christ, a Christian.
Krista		A follower of Christ, a Christian.
Kristabel		Beautiful Christian. Derived from Christina and Belle.
Kristal		Clear as ice. A gemstone name.
Kristel		A follower of Christ, a Christian.
Kristen	Danish	A follower of Christ, a Christian.
Kristie		A follower of Christ, a Christian.
Kristina		A follower of Christ, a Christian.
Kristine		A follower of Christ, a Christian.
Kristy		A follower of Christ, a Christian.
Kriti	Hindu	A work of art.
Krupa	Hindu	
Krupali	Hindu	
Krystal		Clear as ice. A gemstone name.
Krystle		Clear as ice. A gemstone name.
Kshama	Hindu	forgiveness, patience, a form of the Devi.
Kuhuk	Hindu	
Kumari	Sanskrit	A girl or daughter.
Kumud	Hindu	
Kunti	Hindu	Pritha.
Kura	Polynesian/Maori	Polynesian: Red. Maori: Treasure.
Kusum	Hindu	
Kyeema	Aboriginal	Of the dawn, or a Kangaroo.
Kyla	Scottish Gaelic	From the narrow strait. Feminine of Kyle.
Kyleigh		From the narrow strait. Feminine of Kyle.
Kylie	Aboriginal	A boomerang.
Kym		From the meadow.
Kyna	Irish Gaelic	Wise.
Kynthia	Greek	Born under the sign of cancer.
Kyoko	Japanese	A mirror.
Kyon	Korean	Brightness.
Kyra	sun	

Kyrena		A woman from Cyrene, an ancient Greek colony in North Africa.
Kyrenia		A woman from Cyrene, an ancient Greek colony in North Africa.
Lacey	Old French	Lace.
Lae	Laos	Dark.
Laetitia	Latin	Happiness.
Laila		As intoxicating as wine.
Lailie	Hebrew	Born during light.
Laina		Route or path.
Laine		The light of the sun.
Lainey		The light of the sun.
Lakeisha	Swahili	Favorite one.
Lakota	Native American	friend
Lakshmi	Sanskrit	A lucky omen. The Hindu goddess of beauty and wealth.
Lala	Slavonic	A tulip.
Lalage	Greek	Chatter, babble.
Lalasa	Hindu	Love.
Lali		The well-spoken one.
Lalima	Hindu	
Lalita	Sanskrit	Playful, charming.
Lalo	Latin	To sing a lullaby.
Lamilla	Aboriginal	A stone.
Lamorna	Cornish	A location.
Lan	Vietnamese	Flower name.
Lana	English	Afloat, calm as still waters.
Lanai		Terrace, veranda.
Lanaya		Lime tree.
Lane	Old English	From the narrow road.
Lanelle		From the narrow road.
Lanette		
Lani	Polynesian	The sky.
Lanikai	Hawaiian	Heavenly sea.
Laquetta	Native American	
Lara	Russian	Cheerful, light-hearted.
Laraine	Old German	From a province on the border of France and Germany.

Lareine	Old German	From a province on the border of France and Germany.
Lareyne	Old German	From a province on the border of France and Germany.
Lari	English	Crowned with laurel.
Laria	Greek	the sars are mine
Larissa	Russian from Greek	Cheerful, light-hearted.
Lark	English/Aboriginal	English A songbird. Aboriginal a cloud.
Lasca	Latin	Weary.
Lassie	English/Scottish	A little girl.
Lastri	Indonesian	A common girl's name.
Lata	Hindu	
Lateefah	North African	Gentle, pleasant.
Latifa	Arabic	Kind and gentle.
Latisha		Happiness.
Latonia	Latin	In Roman mythology, the mother of Diana.
Latoya	Spanish	Victorious. A popular name in the USA.
Latrice		
Laura	Latin	A laurel wreath or a tree.
Laurel		A laurel wreath or a tree.
Lauren	English	A free person. A feminine form of Charles, Also see Carla, Carol and Caroline.
Laurinda	Latin	Crowned with laurel, praise.
Lavani	Hindu	Grace.
Laveda	Latin	One who is purified or innocent.
Lavender	English from Latin	From the herb.
Laverne	French	Springlike, or from the Alder tree.
Lavinia	Latin	A lady, or a mother of Rome.
Lawrencia		From the Laurel tree or crowned with laurels.
Laxmi	Hindu	Lakshmi.
Layla	Arabic	As intoxicating as wine.
Layna	Greek	Light, truth.
Leah	Irish Gaelic	The light of the sun. Also see Eileen, Elaine, Eleanor and Ellen.
Leala	French	The loyal one.
Leandra	Latin	Like a lioness. The female version of Leander.

Leanna		Graceful willow.
Leanne	English	Grace, or favored by God. A modern invention formed from Lee and Anne.
Leauna		Young deer, fawn.
Leba	Yiddish	Beloved.
Leda	Greek	A mythological queen and the mother of Helen of Troy.
Ledah	Hebrew	Birth.
Lee	Old English	A meadow or clearing.
Leea		Languid, weary. The wife of Jacob in the Bible.
Leela	Sanskrit	Playful.
Leena	Aboriginal	A possum.
Leewana	Aboriginal	The wind.
Lehana	African	One who refuses.
Leigh	Old English	A meadow or clearing.
Leiko	Japanese	Arrogant.
Leila	Arabic	Dark as the night.
Leilani	Hawaiian	A heavenly flower.
Lemana	Aboriginal	The She-Oak tree.
Lemuela	Hebrew	Devoted to God. The feminine form of Lemuel.
Lena	English	From the name Caroline, Helen and other names. Caroline - A free person.
Lene	Dutch/German	A nickname for Helen and Magdalene. Helen - The light of the sun. Magdalene - A woman from the village of Magdala.
Lenis	Latin	Gentle and smooth.
Lenora		The light of the sun. A form of Helen.
Lenore		The light of the sun. A form of Helen.
Leoda	Teutonic	A woman of the people.
Leola	Latin	Lion.
Leoma	Old English	Light, bright.
Leona	Latin	A lioness. A feminine form of Leo or Leon.
Leonarda	Old French	A brave lioness. Feminine form of Leonard.
Leonora		The light of the sun. A form of Helen.

Leontine	Latin	Like a lion.
Leopolda	Old German	Bold leader.
Leora	Greek	Light.
Lesh	Shea	
Lesley	Scottish Gaelic	From an ancient surname.
Letha	Greek	The river of forgetfulness. From the name Lethe.
Leticia		Happiness.
Letitia	Latin	Joy.
Lettice		Happiness.
Leura	Aboriginal	Lava.
Levana	Latin	The rising sun.
Levina	Old English	A bright flash.
Lewanna	Hebrew	The moon.
Lexie		The defender, or helper of mankind. Feminine form of Alexander. Also see Alexis.
Lexine		The defender, or helper of mankind.
Lexy		The defender, or helper of mankind.
Leyna	Old German	Little angel.
Lhamu	Tibetan/Sherpa	A goddess.
Lia	Italian	Languid, weary.
Liadan	Irish	Grey lady.
Lian	Chinese	A graceful willow.
Liana	French	To bind like a vine.
Liani	Spanish	
Liannaka		Bringer of Peace, hope.
Libby		From the name Elizabeth and Sybil.
Liberty	English	Freedom.
Lida	Czech	A woman from Lydia, cultured woman.
Lidia		A woman from Lydia, cultured woman.
Lien	Chinese	A lotus.
Liese	German	Form of Elizabeth, meaning consecrated to God.
Liesl	German	Form of Elizabeth, meaning consecrated to God.
Lila		The beautiful temptress.
Lilac	Persian	Mauve flower.

Lilah	Hebrew	The beautiful temptress.
Lili		Consecrated to God.
Lilia	Russian/Slavonic	Mauve flower. From the name Lilac.
Lilith	Arabic/Hebrew	Dark, a woman of the night.
Lilli		From the name Elizabeth, meaning consecrated to God.
Lillian	English	From the name Elizabeth, meaning consecrated to God.
Lily	Latin	From the flower name, a symbol of purity. Also see Lillian.
Limber	African	Joyfulness.
Lina	Arabic	Tender.
Linda	Spanish	Pretty. Also a nickname from Belinda.
Lindall		A waterfall. Also, a nickname from names like Carolyn.
Lindley	Old English	From the Lime tree meadow.
Lindon	Old English	From the hill of the Lime trees.
Lindsey	Scottish	From an old surname.
Lindy	Spanish	Pretty. Also a nickname from Belinda.
Linette		Idol, bird.
Linh		
Linley	Old English	From the field of Flax.
Linne	Scandinavian	
Linnea	Old Norse	A Lime tree or Lime blossom.
Linnet	Old French	From the name of the small bird.
Linzi	Scottish	From an old surname.
Liora	Liorre, Liorra, Liore	
Lisa		A nickname for Elizabeth, meaning consecrated to God.
Lisabet		Consecrated to God.
Lisabeth		Consecrated to God.
Lisbet		Consecrated to God.
Lisbeth		Consecrated to God.
Lisette		Consecrated to God.
Lissa	Greek	The honeybee.
Lita		The little winged one.
Litsa	Greek	One who brings good news.

Liv		An Olive tree or branch. A symbol of peace. From the name Olivia.
Livana		Lunar.
Livi		An Olive tree or branch. A symbol of peace. From the name Olivia.
Livia		An Olive tree or branch. A symbol of peace. From the name Olivia.
Liz		Consecrated to God.
Liza		Consecrated to God.
Lizbeth		Consecrated to God.
Lizette		Consecrated to God.
Lizzie		Consecrated to God. Also see Isabel and Lisa.
Lizzy		Consecrated to God.
Llv	Old Norse	Defense, protection.
Lodema	Old English	A guide or leader.
Lois	Greek	Agreeable. A name from the New Testament.
Lokelani	Hawaiian	Small red rose.
Lola	Spanish	Sorrow.
Lolaksi	Hindu	A Sakti of Ganesha.
Lona	English/Spanish	Solitary.
Lonikie	pretty one	
Loorea	Aboriginal	The moon.
Lora	German	A laurel wreath or a tree.
Lore	German	A laurel wreath or a tree.
Lorelei	German	Alluring. The name of the river goddess who lured sailors to their death.
Lorelle	Latin	Little. Also see Laura.
Loren	Latin	From the Laurel tree or crowned with laurels.
Lorena		A laurel wreath or a tree.
Lorene		A free person.
Loretta	Italian	A laurel wreath or a tree.
Lori		A laurel wreath or a tree.
Lorie		Crowned with laurels.
Lorinda		
Loris		A laurel wreath or a tree.

Lorna	English/Scottish	Invented by R D Blackmore for the heroine of his 1860s novel Lorna Doone, and possibly derived, from a Scottish location.
Lorrae	Australian	From Lorraine and Rae. From a province on the border of France and Germany.
Lorraine	Old German	From a province on the border of France and Germany.
Lorretta		A laurel wreath or a tree.
Lotta		A free person.
Lotte		Womanly, full grown.
Lottie		A free person.
Lotty		A free person.
Lotus	Greek	The lotus flower.
Louella	English	A famous warrior. A modern name derived from Louise and Ella.
Louisa		A famous warrior.
Louise	Teutonic	A famous warrior maiden. The feminine form of Louis.
Lourdes	French/Spanish	From the pilgrimage town in Southern France.
Love	Old English	Loved one.
Loveday	Old English	Dear day.
Lowan	Aboriginal	A male fowl.
Lowanna	Aboriginal	A girl.
Lowenna	Cornish	Joyful.
Luana	Old German	A graceful warrior maiden.
Luba	Russian/Slavonic	A lover.
Luce		From the name Lucus. A woman from Lucania.
Lucetta	Italian/Spanish	Light. The feminine form of Lucius and Luke.
Lucia	Italian/Spanish	Light. The feminine form of Lucius and Luke.
Lucian	Latin	Person of Light.
Luciana	Italian	Light. The feminine form of Lucius and Luke.
Lucianna	English	A modern combination of Lucy and Anna. Lucy - Light. Anna - Grace, or favored by God.
Lucie		Light. The feminine form of Lucius and Luke.

Lucille		Light. The feminine form of Lucius and Luke.
Lucina	Latin	The Roman goddess of childbirth. Also see Lucy.
Lucinda		Light. The feminine form of Lucius and Luke.
Lucine	Armenian	Moon.
Lucretia	Latin	Reward, riches.
Lucy	Latin	Light. The feminine form of Lucius and Luke.
Ludella	Old English	An elf or pixie maiden.
Ludmila	Slavonic	Loved by the people. A character from an opera by Russian composer Glinka.
Luella	Old English	Elfin.
Luisa	Italian/Spanish	A famous warrior maiden. The feminine form of Louis.
Luise	German	A famous warrior maiden. The feminine form of Louis.
Lujuana	Spanish	
Lukina	Ukrainian	Graceful and bright.
Lulu	German	A famous warrior maiden.
Luna	Latin	The moon.
Lupe	Latin	Wolf.
Lurleen		Alluring.
Lurlene		Alluring.
Lurline		Alluring.
Lurnea	Aboriginal	A resting-place.
Luvena	Latin	The little beloved one.
Lychorinda	Italian	From Shakespeare's play Pericles
Lydia	Greek	A woman from Lydia.
Lykaios	Greek	Wolfish, of a wolf, wolf-like.
Lyn	Welsh	Good looking.
Lynda	Spanish	Pretty. Also a nickname from Belinda.
Lyndal	Australian/English	A modern name possibly derived from Lynn and Dale. Lynn - A waterfall. Dale - A valley dweller.
Lynde		From the hill of the Lime trees.
Lyndel		Pretty.
Lyndey	Spanish	Pretty. Also a nickname from Belinda.
Lyndsey	Scottish	From an old surname.

Lynelle		Pretty.
Lynette		From the name of the small bird.
Lynn	Old English/Welsh	Old English: A waterfall. Welsh: Good looking.
Lynna		Waterfall.
Lynne		Pretty.
Lynnea		Pretty.
Lynnette		From the name of the small bird.
Lynsey	Scottish	From an old surname.
Lyra		
Lyris	Greek	She who plays the harp.
Lys	French	A symbol of purity.
Lysa		A nickname for Elizabeth, meaning consecrated to God.
Lysander	Greek	The liberator.
Lysandra	Greek	The liberator.
Lysette		Consecrated to God.
Lystra	Greek	Free.
Maata	Maori	A lady.
Mab	Irish Gaelic	Intoxicating one. A queen in Irish legend.
Mabel	Old French	Amiable, lovable.
Macaria	Greek	A mythological figure.
Machi	Japanese	Ten thousand.
Machiko	Japanese	Child of Machi.
Maddi		A woman from the village of Magdala.
Maddie		A woman from the village of Magdala.
Maddy		A woman from the village of Magdala.
Madeira	Portuguese	An island off the African coast. Also a fortified wine.
Madeleine	French	A woman from the village of Magdala.
Madelia		A woman from the village of Magdala.
Madeline	Hebrew	A woman from the village of Magdala.
Madge		A pearl.
Madhavi	Hindu	
Madhu	Hindu	Honey.
Madhul	Hindu	

Madhulika	Hindu	
Madhur	Hindu	Sweet.
Madhuri	Sanskrit	Sweet.
Madison	Old English	Child of Maud or Matthew.
Madonna	Italian	My lady. From a title of the Virgin Mary.
Madra	Spanish	Mother.
Madrona	Latin	A lady or noblewoman. A Jewish name.
Madura		An Indonesian island.
Mae		From the name Margaret and Mary. Margaret - A Pearl. Mary - Hebrew: Bitter, as in a bitterly wanted child. Latin: The star of the sea.
Maeve	Irish Gaelic	Intoxicating one. A queen in Irish legend.
Magan	Teutonic	Power.
Magara	Rhodesian	Child of constantl cries.
Magda	German	A woman from the village of Magdala.
Magdalen		A woman from the village of Magdala.
Magdalena		Woman from Magdala.
Magdalene		A woman from the village of Magdala.
Magena	Native American	The coming moon.
Magenta	Italian	A color name, after a town in Italy.
Maggie		A pearl.
Magna	Latin/Norwegian	Latin: Great. Norwegian: Strength.
Magnolia	French	A flower named, after the French botanist Pierre Magnol.
Mahala	Native American, Hebrew, Arabic	Woman, tenderness, marrow.
Mahalia	Hebrew	Tenderness.
Mahdi	African	The expected one.
Mahima	Hindu	
Mahina	Polynesian	The moon.
Mahita	Hindu	
Mahogany		A tree name.
Mahuru	Polynesian	The goddess of Spring.

Name	Origin	Meaning
Mai	Swedish	From the name Margaret and Mary. Margaret - A Pearl. Mary - Hebrew: Bitter, as in a bitterly wanted child. Latin: The star of the sea.
Maia	Hebrew/Latin	Hebrew: Bitter, as in a bitterly wanted child. Latin: The star of the sea. Also see Mars, Marilyn, Marina, Marion, Marlene, Miriam, Moira and Maureen.
Maida	Old English	A maiden.
Maiko	Japanese	Child of Mai.
Maine	French	
Mair	Welsh	Bitter, as in a bitterly wanted child. Also - The star of the sea.
Maire	Irish Gaelic	Bitter, as in a bitterly wanted child. Also - The star of the sea.
Mairead	Irish/Scottish	A pearl.
Mairin	Irish Gaelic	Form of Maureen. Bitter, as in a bitterly wanted child. Also - The star of the sea.
Maisie	Scottish	A pearl. From the name Margaret, but also used independently.
Maitane	Old English	Beloved.
Maitryi	Hindu	Friendship.
Maiya	Aboriginal	A vegetable.
Maizah	African	Discerning.
Maj	Swedish	Pearl.
Majella	Italian	From the name of an Italian saint.
Majesta	Latin	The majestic one.
Majida	Arabic	The illustrious one.
Majondra	Majie, Maj, Jondra	
Makani	Hawaiian	The wind.
Makiko	Japanese	Child of Maki.
Mala		A woman from the village of Magdala.
Malak	Arabic	An angel.
Malati	Sanskrit	A jasmine flower.
Malavika	Hindu	
Malaya	Spanish	Free. Also a country name.
Malca	Hebrew	Queen.
Malena		A woman from the village of Magdala.

Mali	Thai	A flower.
Maliha	Hindu	Strong, beautiful.
Malika	Arabic	The feminine form of Malik, the master.
Malila	Miwok Indian	Salmon going fast upstream.
Malina	Hebrew, Hindu	tower, dark
Malise	Scottish Gaelic	The servant of God.
Malka	Hebrew	Queen.
Malkah	Hebrew	A queen.
Mallana	Aboriginal	A canoe.
Mallika	Hindu	
Mallory	Old French	Unlucky.
Malu	Hawaiian	Peacefulness.
Malva	Greek	Soft and tender.
Malvina	Gaelic	The smooth-browed one.
Mamiko	Japanese	Child of Mami.
Mamta	Hindu	Mother's love for child, wife of sage Asija.
Manasi	Hindu	
Manavi	Hindu	
Manda		Worthy of being loved.
Mandara	Hindu	Mythical tree.
Mandeep	Hindu	Light of heart.
Mandie		Worthy of being loved.
Mandisa	African	Sweet.
Mandy		Worthy of being loved.
Mangena	Hebrew	Melody.
Manhattan	Old English, Scottish	Whiskey.
Mani	Aboriginal/Sanskrit	Aboriginal: Equal. Sanskrit: A jewel.
Manilla	Aboriginal	A winding river.
Manisha	Hindu	sharp intellect, genius, sagacity
Manjari	Hindu	
Manju	Hindu	
Manjula	Hindu	
Manjusha	Sanskrit	A box of jewels.
Manon	French	Bitter, as in a bitterly wanted child, the star of the sea.
Mansi	Hopi Indian	Plucked flower.
Manuela	Spanish	God is with us. Feminine form of Emmanuel.

Manuella		God is with us. Feminine form of Emmanuel.
Manuelle		God is with us. Feminine form of Emmanuel.
Manushi	Hindu	
Manya	Aboriginal	Small.
Mara	Hebrew	Bitter. The original form of Mary.
Marabel		A combination of Mary and Belle.
Marcella	Latin	Belonging to Mars. The feminine form of Marcus or Mark.
Marcia	Latin	Belonging to Mars.
Marcie		From the name Marcia. Belonging to Mars.
Marcy		From the name Marcia. Belonging to Mars.
Mardi	French	Born on a Tuesday.
Mare		The sea.
Marea	Hebrew/Latin	Hebrew: Bitter, as in a bitterly wanted child. Latin: The star of the sea. Also see Mars, Marilyn, Marina, Marion, Marlene, Miriam, Moira and Maureen.
Maree	Hebrew/Latin	Hebrew: Bitter, as in a bitterly wanted child. Latin: The star of the sea. Also see Mars, Marilyn, Marina, Marion, Marlene, Miriam, Moira and Maureen.
Marelda	Teutonic	A famous battle maiden.
Maren	Latin	Sea.
Maresa		Of the sea. Also see Marina and Mary.
Margaret	Latin	A pearl. Also see Margot, Marguerite, Megan.
Margarita	Spanish	A pearl.
Marge		A pearl.
Margo	French	Pearl.
Margot	French	Originally a nickname from Margaret, but now an independent name.
Marguerite	French	A pearl.
Mari		Wished-for child.

Maria	Hebrew/Latin	Hebrew: Bitter, as in a bitterly wanted child. Latin: The star of the sea. Also see Mars, Marilyn, Marina, Marion, Marlene, Miriam, Moira and Maureen.
Mariabella	Italian	my beautiful Mary
Mariah	Hebrew/Latin	Hebrew: Bitter, as in a bitterly wanted child. Latin: The star of the sea. Also see Mars, Marilyn, Marina, Marion, Marlene, Miriam, Moira and Maureen.
Mariam	Hebrew	Wished-for child.
Mariamne	Hebrew	The Hebrew form of Miriam.
Marian	French/Polish	Bitter, as in a bitterly wanted child, the star of the sea.
Mariana	French	Bitter, as in a bitterly wanted child, the star of the sea.
Marianne	French	Bitter, as in a bitterly wanted child, the star of the sea.
Mariasha	Egyptian, Hebrew	Perfect one, bitter, with sorrow.
Maribel	Spanish	A combination of Maria and Belle or Isabel.
Maribeth		Bitter sea, house of God.
Maricel	Latin	Full of grace.
Marie	French	A biblical name meaning bitter.
Marieke	Dutch	A biblical name meaning bitter.
Mariel		Bitter, as in a bitterly wanted child, the star of the sea.
Marielle	French	Bitter, as in a bitterly wanted child. Also - The star of the sea.
Marietta	Italian	Bitter, as in a bitterly wanted child. Also - The star of the sea.
Marigold	Old English	A golden flower.
Marika	Maori/Slavonic	Maori: Quiet and careful. Slavonic: A biblical name meaning bitter.
Mariko	Japanese	child of Mari
Marilee	Greek	bitterness
Marilyn		Bitter, as in a bitterly wanted child, the star of the sea.
Marina	Latin	Of the sea.
Marinel		Of the sea.
Marinka	Russian	Of the sea. Derived from Marina.
Marinna	Aboriginal	A song.
Mariola		

Marion	Old French from Latin	Bitter, as in a bitterly wanted child. Also - The star of the sea.
Mariposa	Spanish	Butterfly.
Mariquita	Spanish	Bitter, as in a bitterly wanted child, the star of the sea.
Maris	Latin	Of the sea.
Marisa		Of the sea.
Marisela		From the sea.
Marisol		Sunny sea.
Marissa		Of the sea.
Marita	Spanish	Bitter, as in a bitterly wanted child, the star of the sea.
Marjani	Swahili	Coral.
Marjeta	Czech	Pearl.
Marjorie	English	Derived from Margaret, an English name meaning Pearl.
Marketta	Finnish	Finnish form of Margaret.
Marla	Hebrew/Latin	Hebrew: Bitter, as in a bitterly wanted child. Latin: The star of the sea.
Marlee	Aboriginal	An Elder tree. Also see Marlene.
Marlene	German	
Marliss		
Marlon	Old French	Wild falcon.
Marly		
Marmara	Greek	Radiant.
Marna	Hebrew	Rejoice.
Marne		From the name Marina. Marina - Of the sea.
Marnie		From the name Marina. Marina - Of the sea.
Marnina	Hebrew	Cause of joy.
Marny	Scandinavian	From the sea.
Marsala	Italian	A town, and a sweet fortified wine.
Marsha	Latin	Belonging to Mars. Also see Marcella.
Marta	Italian/Spanish	A lady.
Martha	Aramaic	A lady. A name from the Bible.
Martina	Latin	Of Mars, the Roman god of war. The feminine form of Martin.
Maru	Polynesian	Gentle.

Maruti	Hindu	
Marvel	Latin	A wonderful thing.
Marvela		Marvelous.
Marvelle	Old French	Miracle.
Mary	Hebrew/Latin	Hebrew: Bitter. Latin: The star of the sea.
Mary-Ellen		Hebrew: Bitter. Latin: The star of the sea.
Mary-Jane		Hebrew: Bitter. Latin: The star of the sea.
Maryam	Arabic	A biblical name meaning bitter. Also see Mary.
Maryann		Hebrew: Bitter. Latin: The star of the sea.
Marylou		Hebrew: Bitter. Latin: The star of the sea.
Maryvonne	French	Hebrew: Bitter. Latin: The star of the sea.
Masa	Japanese	Good and straightforward.
Masako	Japanese	Child of Masa.
Matana	Arabic	Gift.
Matangi	Hindu	A Devi.
Mathea	Hebrew	Gift of God.
Mathilda	Old German	Battle maiden, strength.
Matilda	Teutonic	The mighty battle maiden.
Matrika	Hindu	Mother, name of goddess.
Matsu	Japanese	A Pine tree.
Mattea	Hebrew	The gift of God. The feminine form of Matthew.
Matty		The mighty battle maiden.
Maud		The mighty battle maiden.
Maude		The mighty battle maiden.
Maura	Celtic	The name of a 5th-century saint.
Maureen		Bitter, as in a bitterly wanted child. Also - The star of the sea.
Mavis	French	A songbird.
Maxim		The greatest. The feminine form of Maximilian.
Maxima		Miracle worker.
Maxime		The greatest. The feminine form of Maximilian.
Maxine	Latin	The greatest. The feminine form of Maximilian.

May		A month.
Maya	Latin	The great one. The name of a Roman goddess and a Hindu goddess. Also a nickname from Maria.
Mayako	Japanese	Child of Maya.
Maybelle		Amiable, lovable.
Maye		
Mayoko	Japanese	Child of Mayo.
Mayrah	Aboriginal	Spring, or the wind.
Maysa	Arabic	She who walks gracefully.
Mayuko	Japanese	Child of Mayu.
Mayuri	Hindu	
Meagin		
Meckenzie	Gaelic	Daughter of the Wise Leader
Meda	Native American	Priestess.
Medea	Greek	The name of a princess in classical mythology.
Medha	Hindu	Intelligence, a form of the Devi.
Medilion		
Medina	Arabic	The name of a city in Saudi Arabia.
Medusa	Greek	A character from mythology.
Mee	Chinese	Beautiful.
Meena	Sanskrit	Fish. The name represents the zodiac sign Pisces.
Meenakshi	Hindu	
Meera	Aboriginal	A string bag.
Meg		A pearl. Form of Margaret.
Megan	Welsh	A pearl. Form of Margaret.
Megara	Greek	A mythological figure.
Meggie		A pearl. Form of Margaret.
Megha	Hindu	
Meghana	Hindu	Raincloud.
Mehitabel	Hebrew	God is our joy.
Mei	Latin	Great one.
Meinwen	Welsh	Fair and slender.
Meira	Hebrew	Light.
Mekia		
Mela	Hindu	Religious gathering.
Melanctha	Greek	Black flower.

Melanie	Greek	The dark or black one.
Melantha	Greek	The dark flower.
Melba	English	After the famous singer Dame Nellie Melba. She named herself after her home town, Melbourne Australia.
Melda		A floret.
Melek	Arabic	An angel.
Melia	Greek	A mythological nymph.
Melina	Greek	Gentle.
Melinda	English	From Melanie and Linda. Melanie - The dark or black one. Linda - Pretty.
Melisanda		Strong and industrious.
Melisande	French	Strong and industrious.
Melisenda	Spanish	honest, diligent
Melissa	Greek	The honeybee.
Mell		Industrious, striving.
Melli		Industrious, striving.
Mellie		Industrious, striving.
Mellissa	Greek	The honeybee.
Melly		Industrious, striving.
Melody	Greek	Like a song.
Melosa	Spanish	Gentle, sweet.
Melva	Welsh	A sweet place.
Melvina		Armored chief.
Melwyn	Cornish	As fair as honey.
Mena	Hindu	Mother of Menaka.
Menaka	Hindu	Celestial damsel.
Menuha	Hebrew	Tranquility.
Mercedes	Spanish	Merciful. From a title of the Virgin Mary.
Mercy	Middle English	Compassion, pity.
Mere	Polynesian	Bitter, as in a bitterly wanted child. Also - The star of the sea.
Meredith	Old Welsh	A lord.
Meriel		Of the bright sea.
Merilyn		
Merinda	Aboriginal	A beautiful woman.
Meris		Of the sea.
Merisa		Of the sea.

Merissa		Of the sea.
Merit	Latin	Deserving.
Merivale	Old English	A pleasant valley.
Merle	Old French	A blackbird.
Merlin	Old Welsh	From the fort by the sea, or the falcon, a wizard.
Merlyn	Old Welsh	From the fort by the sea, or the falcon, a wizard.
Merpati	Indonesian	A dove.
Merri	Aboriginal	A stone.
Merrill	Old English	Of the bright sea. Also joyful, happy.
Merry	Old English	Joyful, happy.
Merryn	Cornish	The name of a saint and a village.
Mersadize	Sadize	
Mertice	Old English	Pleasant and famous.
Meryl		A blackbird. Also a nickname for Meriel.
Meryle		A blackbird. Also a nickname for Meriel.
Mesha	Hindu	Ram, born under the sign of Aries
Messina	Latin	The middle child.
Meta	Latin	The ambitious one.
Metis	Greek	The wise one.
Mia	Scandinavian	Bitter, as in a bitterly wanted child. Also - The star of the sea.
Miah	Aboriginal	The moon.
Miakoda	Native American	Power of the moon.
Michaela	Hebrew	Feminine form of Michael. Like the Lord.
Michal	Hebrew	A brook. A biblical name.
Michel	French	Feminine form of Michael.
Michele	French	Feminine form of Michael.
Micheline		Who is like God.
Michelle	French from Hebrew	Like the Lord. A feminine form of Michael.
Michi	Japanese	Righteous.
Michiko	Japanese	Child of Michi.
Micki		Feminine form of Michael. Like the Lord.

Mickie		Feminine form of Michael. Like the Lord.
Micky		Feminine form of Michael. Like the Lord.
Midori	Japanese	Green.
Migina	Omaha Indian	Moon returning.
Mignon	French	Sweet and dainty.
Mignonette		Sweet and dainty.
Mihoko	Japanese	Child of Mihoko.
Mika	Japanese	The new moon.
Miki	Aboriginal/Japanese	Aboriginal: The moon. Japanese: A stem.
Mikki		From the name Michaela. Like the Lord.
Mildred	Old English	Strong yet gentle.
Milena	Czech	The favored one.
Mili		Who is for me?
Milli		Industrious, striving.
Millicent	Teutonic	Strong and industrious.
Millie		Industrious, striving.
Milly		Industrious, striving.
Mily	Hawaiian	Beautiful.
Mimi	Italian	Bitter, as in a bitterly wanted child. Also - The star of the sea.
Mimosa	Latin	A plant name.
Min	Korean	Cleverness.
Mina	Japanese	South.
Minako	Japanese	Child of Mina.
Mincarlie	Aboriginal	Rain.
Minda	Native American	Knowledge.
Mindel	Yiddish	Sea of bitterness.
Mindy		Honey.
Mine	Japanese	A resolute protector.
Minelli		
Minerva	Latin	The mythological goddess of wisdom.
Minette		From the name Mignonette. Sweet and dainty.
Mingmei	Chinese	Smart, beautiful.
Minka	Teutonic	Strong, resolute.
Minna	Teutonic	Love.

Minnie		The resolute protector. A feminine form of William.
Minta	Greek	Of the mint plant.
Mira	Slavonic	The famous one. Also see Myra.
Mirabel		Of uncommon beauty.
Mirabelle	Latin	Lovely.
Miranda	Latin	The admired one. Invented by Shakespeare for the heroine of The Tempest.
Miremba	Ugandan	Peace.
Mireya	Spanish	Miraculous.
Miriam	Hebrew	A biblical name meaning bitter. Also see Mary.
Miriyan	Aboriginal	A star.
Mirrin	Aboriginal	A cloud.
Misako	Japanese	Child of Misa.
Misha		Feminine form of Michael. Like the Lord.
Missy	Old English	Young girl.
Misty	Old English	Of the mist.
Mitena	Native American	Coming moon, new moon.
Mitexi	Native American	Sacred moon.
Mitsuko	Japanese	Child of Mitsu.
Mitzi	Swiss	Bitter, as in a bitterly wanted child. Also - The star of the sea.
Miyoko	Japanese	beautiful generations child
Modestus	Latin	Modest one.
Modesty	Latin	The moderate or modest one.
Mohana	Sanskrit	Bewitching. The enchantress.
Mohini	Hindu	most beautiful
Moina		The noble one.
Moira	Irish Gaelic	Bitter, as in a bitterly wanted child. Also - The star of the sea.
Mollie		Bitter, as in a bitterly wanted child. Also - The star of the sea.
Molly		Bitter, as in a bitterly wanted child. Also - The star of the sea.
Momoko	Japanese	Child of Momo.
Mona	Irish Gaelic	The noble one. Also a nickname from Monica.
Monica	Latin	An adviser or counselor.
Moon	Korean	Letters.

Mora	Spanish	Blueberry.
Morag	Scottish Gaelic	The great one.
Moree	Aboriginal	Water or a spring.
Moreen		Bitter, as in a bitterly wanted child. Also - The star of the sea.
Morenwyn	Cornish	A fair maiden.
Morgan	Welsh	The bright sea.
Morgana		Seashore.
Morgance	Celtic	Sea-dweller.
Morgandy	Celtic	Little one from the edge of the sea.
Morgen	German	Morning.
Moria	Hebrew	My teacher is God.
Morilla	Aboriginal	From the stony ridge.
Morna		Beloved.
Morva	Cornish	From a location.
Morven	Gaelic	A Scottish region.
Morwenna	Cornish/Welsh	A maiden.
Moselle	French from Egyptian	Probably meaning born of. The feminine form of Moses.
Moya		The noble one.
Moyna		Bitter, as in a bitterly wanted child. Also - The star of the sea.
Mridul	Hindu	
Mridula	Hindu	
Mrinalini	Hindu	
Muna	Arabic	A hope, or a wish.
Munira	Arabic	The luminous one.
Mura	Japanese	From the village.
Muriel	Gaelic	Of the bright sea.
Murphy	Irish Gaelic	A warrior of the sea.
Musetta	Greek	A little muse.
Mutsuko	Japanese	Child of Mutsu.
Muzaffer	Turkish	
My-Duyen	Vietnamese	Beautiful, pretty.
Mya	Burmese	Emerald.
Mychau	Vietnamese	Great.
Myfanwy	Welsh	The beloved one.
Myiesha	Arabic	Life's blessing
Mykala		

Myndee	Aboriginal	A sycamore.
Myra	Greek	Fragrant. From myrrh, an aromatic shrub.
Myriam		A biblical name meaning bitter. Also see Mary.
Myrna	Irish Gaelic	Beloved.
Myron	Greek	Fragrant. From myrrh, an aromatic shrub.
Myrtle	Greek	A plant name.
Myuna	Aboriginal	Clear water.
Nabelung	African	Beautiful one.
Nabila	Arabic	Noble.
Nada	Arabic	The generous one.
Nadda	Aboriginal	A camp.
Nadezda	Czech	One with hope.
Nadia	Slavonic	Hope.
Nadie		Hope.
Nadine		Hope.
Nadira	Arabic	Precious.
Nadya		The generous one.
Nafeeza	Arabic	Precious thing.
Nagihan	Turkish	
Nahoko	Japanese	Child of Naho.
Naia	Greek	Flowing.
Naida	Greek	A water nymph.
Nailah	African	Succeeding.
Naimah	Arabic	Living a soft, enjoyable life.
Naina	Hindu	Eyes.
Nairne	Scottish Gaelic	From the river.
Nalani	Hawaiian	The calm of the skies.
Nalini	Sanskrit	Lovely.
Nama	Aboriginal	A Tea-Tree.
Namazzi	Ugandan	Water.
Nami	Japanese	A wave.
Namiko	Japanese	Child of Nami.
Namrata	Hindu	
Nan		Grace, or favored by God.
Nanako	Japanese	Child of Nana.
Nancy		Grace, or favored by God. Originally a nickname from Anne, but also an independent name.

Nandini	Hindu	
Nandita	Hindu	
Nanette	French	Grace, or favored by God. Originally a nickname from Anne, but also an independent name.
Nani	Polynesian	Beautiful.
Nanine		Grace, or favored by God. From the Hebrew name Hannah,.
Nanna	Hebrew	Graceful one.
Nanon	French	Grace, or favored by God. From the name Anne.
Nantale	Ugandan	clan totem is a lion
Naoko	Japanese	child of Nao
Naomi	Hebrew	Pleasant. A biblical name, and the feminine form of Noam.
Napea	Latin	A girl of the valley.
Nara	Old English/Japanese/Aboriginal	Old English: The nearest and dearest one. Japanese: An Oak tree. Aboriginal: A companion.
Narcissa	Greek	Self-love.
Narda	Latin	A fragrant ointment or perfume.
Narella	Greek	Bright one.
Narelle	Australian	Old English: The nearest and dearest one. Japanese: An Oak tree. Aboriginal: A companion. Elle - She, a woman.
Naretha	Aboriginal	A saltbush.
Narkeasha	African	Pretty.
Narmada	Hindu	Name of a river.
Nasha	African	Born during rainy season.
Nashwa	Egyptian	Wonderful feeling.
Nasiche	Ugandan	Born during locust season.
Nasrin	Persian	A wild rose.
Nastasia	Russian from Greek	She who will rise again.
Natala		Born at Christmas. From the name Natalie, but also used as an independent name.
Natalia		Born at Christmas. From the name Natalie, but also used as an independent name.
Natalie	Latin	Born at Christmas.
Natalya	Russian	Born at Christmas.
Natane	Native American	Female child.

Nataniella	Hebrew	Gift of God.
Natasha	Russian	Born at Christmas. From the name Natalie, but also used as an independent name.
Nathalie	French	Born at Christmas. From the name Natalie, but also used as an independent name.
Nathania	Hebrew	The gift of God. Feminine form of Nathan.
Natividad	Spanish	The nativity.
Natsuko	Japanese	Child of Natsu.
Navdeep	Hindu	
Naveena	Hindu	Strong-willed supporter.
Nawal	Arabic	A gift.
Nayoko	Japanese	Child of Nayo.
Naysa	Hebrew	miracle of God
Nazaret	Spanish	Of Nazareth.
Nazirah	Arabic	equal, like
Nea		New, the newcomer.
Neala	Irish Gaelic	The champion. Feminine form of Neal or Neil.
Neci	Latin	Intense, fiery.
Neda	Slavonic	Born on Sunday.
Nediva	Hebrew	Noble and generous.
Neeharika	Hindu	
Neelam	Hindu	Sapphire.
Neelja	Hindu	
Neena	Hindu	
Neerja	Hindu	Lotus flower.
Neeta	Hindu	
Neha	Hindu	Rain.
Neka	Native American	A wild goose.
Nelda	Old English	Of the Elder tree.
Nelia		The champion.
Nell	Old French	The light of the sun. From Eleanor and a form of Helen.
Nelleke	Dutch	A horn.
Nellie		From Helen.
Nellwyn	Old English	A bright companion.
Neola	Greek	The young one.
Neoma	Greek	The new moon.

Nerhim	Turkish	
Neria	Hebrew	Lamp of God, angel.
Nerida	Aboriginal	A flower.
Nerin	Greek	One from the sea.
Nerina	Greek	A sea nymph.
Nerissa	Greek	A sea nymph.
Neroli		After an Italian princess.
Nerys	Welsh	A lady.
Nessa		Pure, chaste.
Nessan		Stoat.
Nesta	Welsh	Pure, chaste. Form of Agnes.
Netanya		God's gift.
Netta	Latin	Beyond price, praiseworthy.
Nettie	Latin	Beyond price, praiseworthy.
Netty	Latin	Beyond price, praiseworthy.
Neva	Spanish	Covered with snow.
Nevada	Spanish	Snow, or as white as snow. Also the name of an American state.
Newlyn	Celtic	The dweller at the new pool.
Neysa	Greek	Pure.
Ngaio	Maori	The name of a native New Zealand tree.
Ngaire	Maori	Flaxen.
Nhu	Vietnamese	Everything according to one's wishes.
Nia	Swahili	Purpose.
Niamh	Irish Gaelic	Beautiful, bright. The daughter of a sea god in Irish mythology.
Nichelle		Victorious maiden.
Nicia	Greek	Victorious army.
Nicki		The people's victory. From the name Nicole.
Nickita	Hindu	
Nicola	Latin	The people's victory. The feminine form of Nicholas.
Nicole		Victory of the people.
Nicolette	French	The people's victory. From the name Nicole.
Nidra	Hindu	A form of the Devi.
Niju	Hindu	Pan-sophist.
Nika	Russian	Born on Sunday.

Nike	Greek	Victory.
Nikita	Russian/Greek	Unconquered people.
Nikki		The people's victory. From the name Nicole.
Niley	Aboriginal	A shell.
Nilg?n	Turkish	
Nilima	Hindu	
Nilini	Hindu	Perpetuator of the Kuru race.
Nima	Tibetan/Sherpa	Sun.
Nimah	Arabic	Blessing, loan.
Nimisha	Hindu	
Nimmi	Hindu	
Nimue		
Nina	Spanish	A girl. Also see Anne and Antonia.
Ninon	French	Grace, or favored by God. From the name Anne.
Niobe	Greek	Fern.
Nira	Modern Hebrew	Of the loom.
Niradhara	Hindu	
Niral	Hindu	
Nirguna	Hindu	
Nirvana	Hindu	Deep silence, ultimate bliss.
Nirvelli	Native American	Water child.
Nisha	Hindu	Night.
Nishtha	Hindu	
Nisi	Hebrew	Emblem.
Nissa	Scandinavian	A friendly elf.
Nita	Native American	A bean grower. Feminine form of Fabian.
Nitara	Hindu	Deeply rooted.
Niti	Hindu	
Nitika	Native American	Angel of precious stone.
Nitu	Hindu	
Nitya	Hindu	Goddess Parvati.
Nitzana	Hebrew	Blossom.
Nivedita	Hindu	
Niverta	Hindu	
Nixie	German	A water sprite.
Niyati	Hindu	Fate.
Nizana	Hebrew	A flower bud.

Noelani	Hawaiian	A beautiful girl from heaven.
Noella	French	Christmas.
Noelle	Old French	Christmas, or born at Christmas. The feminine form of Noel.
Nola	Irish Gaelic	The champion, or the fair-shouldered one. Also see Nuala.
Noleen		The people's victory. The feminine form of Nicholas.
Nolene		The people's victory. From the name Nicole.
Noleta	Latin	Unwilling.
Nona	Latin	The ninth, as in the ninth child.
Noni		From the name Nona and Nora. Nona - The ninth, as in the ninth child. Nora - The light of the sun.
Nonie		From the name Nona and Nora. Nona - The ninth, as in the ninth child. Nora - The light of the sun.
Noor	Arabic	Light.
Noora	Aboriginal	A camp.
Nora		The light of the sun.
Norah		The light of the sun.
Norberta	Old German	Blond hero.
Nordica	Teutonic	From the North.
Noreen		The light of the sun.
Nori	Japanese	A doctrine.
Noriko	Japanese	Doctrine child.
Norma	Latin	A rule or standard. The perfect girl or woman. Also a Scottish feminine form of Norman.
Norna	Old Norse	The goddess of fate.
Nova	Greek	New, the newcomer.
Novyanna		Lovely.
Noya	Arabic	Beautiful, ornamented.
Nozomi	Japanese	Hope.
Nu	Burmese	Tender.
Nuala	Irish Gaelic	The fair-shouldered one. Also see Nola.
Nuray	Turkish	White moon.
Nurhan	Turkish	
Nydia	Latin	A refuge or nest.
Nyoko	Japanese	A gem or treasure.

Nyree		Flaxen.
Nyssa	Greek	The beginning.
Nyx	Latin	White-haired.
Oanez	Breton	
Oba	Nigerian	An ancient river goddess.
Obelia	Greek	A pillar or needle.
Octavia	Latin	The eighth.
Oda	Teutonic	Rich.
Odea		Walker by the road.
Odelia	Hebrew	I will praise God.
Odera	Hebrew	Plow.
Odessa	Greek	Along journey.
Odetta		Melody.
Odette	French	A home-lover.
Odile	French	Riches, prosperity. From a medieval German name, and a feminine version of Otto.
Ofelia	Spanish	To help, a helper.
Ofilia		To help, a helper.
Ofra	Hebrew	A fawn, or a lively maiden.
Ofrah	Hebrew	A fawn, or a lively maiden.
Ohanna	Armenian	God's gracious gift
Okalani	Hawaiian	From Heaven.
Okelani	Hawaiian	From Heaven.
Oksana	Russian	Glory be to God.
Ola	Scandinavian	A descendant. The feminine form of Olaf.
Olalla	Spanish	The well-spoken one.
Olathe	Native American	Beautiful.
Olayinka	Yoruban	Honors surround me.
Olba	Aboriginal	Reddish colored.
Olcay	Turkish	
Oleander	Greek	An evergreen tree.
Olena	Ukrainian	The light of the sun.
Olesia	Polish	Helper and defender of mankind.
Olethea	Latin	Truth.
Olga	Russian	The holy one. The name of a 10th-century saint and the feminine form of Oleg.
Oliana	Hawaiian	Oleander.
Olien	Russian	The dear one.

Olinda	Latin	Fragrant.
Olive		An Olive tree or branch. A symbol of peace. Feminine version of Oliver.
Olivia	Latin	An Olive tree or branch. A symbol of peace. Feminine version of Oliver.
Olono	Aboriginal	A hill.
Olva		The holy one.
Olwen	Welsh	White or fair footprints. The name of a character in Welsh legend.
Olya		The holy one.
Olympia	Latin	The heavenly one. From the home of the Gods.
Oma	Arabic	Long-lived. The feminine form of Omar.
Omaka	Maori	The place where the stream flows.
Omega	Greek	The last.
Ona	Lithuanian	Grace, or favored by God.
Onawa	Native American	One who is wide-awake.
Ondine	Latin	A water sprite.
Onenn	Breton	
Onida	Native American	The expected or awaited one.
Onora	Irish Gaelic	Version of Honor.
Onur	Turkish	
Onyx	Greek	A semi-precious stone.
Oola	Aboriginal	A red lizard.
Oona	Irish	
Oonagh	Irish	
Opal	Sanskrit	A jewel, or precious stone.
Opaline	French	A jewel, or precious stone.
Ophelia	Greek	To help, a helper. A character in Shakespeare's Hamlet.
Ophira	Greek	Gold.
Ophrah	Hebrew	A fawn, or a lively maiden.
Ora	Latin/Polynesian	Latin: Light, golden. Polynesian: Life.
Oralee		Golden.
Oralia		Golden.
Oralie		Golden.
Orana	Aboriginal	The moon.

Orane	French	Rising.
Orchid	Latin	A flower name.
Ordelia	Teutonic	The spear of the elf.
Orea	Greek	The maid of the mountains.
Orelia		Golden.
Orenda	Iroquois Indian	Magic power.
Oriana	Latin	To rise. An Italian name.
Orianna	Latin	Golden, dawning.
Oriel		Golden.
Orinda	Teutonic	Fire serpent.
Oriole	Latin	A golden bird.
Orissa		A state in eastern India.
Orla	Irish Gaelic	Golden. Form of Aurelia.
Orlan	Old English	From the pointed land.
Orlanda	Latin	Bright sun.
Orlantha	Old German	From the land.
Orna	Hebrew/Irish Gaelic	Hebrew: Light. Irish Gaelic: Pale.
Ornella	Italian	A flowering Ash tree.
Orpah	Hebrew	A fawn, or a lively maiden.
Orsa		A female bear.
Orseline		A female bear.
Orsola		A female bear.
Ortense	Italian	The garden lover.
Ortensia	Italian	The garden lover.
Orvokki		Finnish form of Violet.
Ottavia	Italian	The eighth.
Ottilie		Riches, prosperity. From a medieval German name, and a feminine version of Otto.
Ottoline		Riches, prosperity. From a medieval German name, and a feminine version of Otto.
Ourania		Heavenly.
Owena	Welsh	Well-born. The feminine form of Owen.
Ozora	Hebrew	The strength of the Lord.
Pacifica	Latin	Calm. Also after the Pacific Ocean.
Padma	Sanskrit	A lotus.
Padmini	Hindu	
Paige	Old English/French	A young child. French: A young attendant or page.

Pakuna	Miwok Indian	deer jumping down hill
Palila	Hawaiian	A bird.
Pallas	Greek	Knowledge and wisdom.
Pallavi	Hindu	
Palma	Latin	A Palm tree. Also the name of a town in Majorca.
Paloma	Spanish from Latin	A dove.
Palomi	Hindu	
Pamee	Hindu	
Pamela	English	A name invented by the 16th-century poet Sir Philip Sidney, possibly based on the Greek word for sweetness or honey.
Pamelia		From the name Pamela.
Pandora	Greek	All-gifted, talented. A figure from Greek mythology.
Pangari	Aboriginal	A shadow, or of the soul.
Pania	Maori	A mythological sea-maiden.
Pankhudi	Hindu	
Pankita	Hindu	
Panna	Hungarian	Grace, or favored by God. Form of Anne.
Pansy	Old French	Thoughts. Also the name of a flower.
Panthea	Greek	All of the gods.
Pantxike	Latin	Free.
Panya	Latin, Swahili	Crowned with laurel, mouse, small child.
Panyin	Ghanese	Older of twins.
Paola	Italian	Small. Feminine form of Paul.
Paolina		Small. Feminine form of Paul.
Papillon	French	Butterfly.
Parisa	Persian	angelic face
Parnella	Old French	A little rock.
Parnika	Hindu	Auspicious.
Parnita	Hindu	Auspicious.
Parthenia	Greek	Maidenly, virginal.
Parthivi	Hindu	The Goddess Sita.
Parul	Hindu	
Parvani	Hindu	Full moon.
Parvati	Sanskrit	The daughter of the mountain.
Parveen	Hindu	Star.

Pasang	Tibetan/Sherpa	Born on a Friday.
Pascale	French from Latin	Easter.
Patia	Spanish	Leaf.
Patience	English	One of the seven virtues.
Patricia	Latin	Noble, well-born. The feminine form of Patrick.
Patsy		Noble, wellborn. From the name Patricia.
Patty		Noble, wellborn. From the name Patricia.
Paula	Latin	Small. Feminine form of Paul.
Paulette	French	Small. Feminine form of Paul.
Paulina	Spanish	Small. Feminine form of Paul.
Pauline	French	Small. Feminine form of Paul.
Paulomi	Hindu	
Pauravi	Hindu	
Pavi	Hindu	
Payal	Hindu	Anklet.
Payge	Old English	A young child.
Paz	Spanish from Latin	Peace.
Pazia	Hebrew	Golden.
Peace	Latin	Peace.
Pearl	Old French	A precious gem.
Pearlie		A precious gem.
Pearly		A precious gem.
Pebbles	English	A stone.
Peg		A pearl.
Pegeen	Greek	A pearl.
Peggie		A pearl.
Peggy		A pearl.
Pelagia	Greek	From the sea.
Pema	Tibetan/Sherpa	A lotus.
Penda	Swahili	Love.
Penelope	Greek	The weaver. A character from Greek mythology.
Pengana	Aboriginal	A hawk.
Peni	Hawaiian	Weaver.
Penina	Hebrew	Jewel, coral.
Penney		The weaver.
Pennie		The weaver.
Penny		The weaver.

Penthea	Greek	The fifth.
Peony	Latin	Healing. A flower name.
Pepa	Spanish	God shall add.
Pepita	Spanish	God shall add.
Pepper	English	From the pepper plant.
Perdita	Latin	The lost one. A name invented by Shakespeare for a character in The Winter's Tale.
Peridot	Arabic	A green gemstone.
Perla	Italian/Spanish	A pearl.
Perle		A pearl.
Perlina		A pearl.
Perouze	Armenian	Turquoise.
Perri	English	Wanderer.
Perry	Old English/French	The dweller by the pear tree. Also from the name Peregrine.
Persephone	Greek	The name of the goddess of the underworld.
Persia		From the name of the country.
Persis	Latin	A woman from Persia.
Peta	Aboriginal/Greek	Aboriginal: A tree. Greek: A rock or stone. A modern feminine form of Peter. Also see Parnella and Petronel.
Petara	Latin	A rock.
Petra	Latin	A rock.
Petronel	Latin	From the name of an early saint, and related to the boy's name Peter.
Petula	English	A modern name possibly derived from the Latin word for 'to ask' or 'to seek'.
Petunia		A flower name.
Phaedra	Greek	The bright one. The wife of Theseus in Greek mythology.
Phebe	Italian	Radiant, bright. The name of a Greek deity.
Phedra	Greek	Shining one.
Phelia		To help, a helper.
Phila		Love.
Philadelphia	Greek	Brotherly love. The name of a city in the USA.
Philana	Greek	A friend of mankind.

Philantha	Greek	A lover of flowers.
Philberta	Old English	Very brilliant.
Philena		Lover of mankind.
Philida		A green bough or branch.
Philippa	Greek	A lover of horses. The feminine form of Philip.
Phillida		A green bough or branch.
Philomela	Greek	A lover of song.
Philomena	Greek	A lover of the moon.
Phoebe	Greek	Radiant, bright. The name of a Greek deity.
Phoena	Greek	Mystical bird, purple.
Phoenix	Greek	The legendary bird that rose again from its own ashes.
Phoolan	Hindu	Flower.
Photini		Light.
Phrynia		From Shakespeare's play Timon of Athens.
Phuong	Vietnamese	Destiny.
Phutika	Hindu	
Phylicia		Happiness.
Phyliss	Greek	A green bough or branch.
Phyllida		A green bough or branch.
Phyllis	Greek	A green bough or branch.
Pia	Latin	Pious, devout. An Italian and Spanish name.
Pier	Aboriginal/Greek	Aboriginal: A tree. Greek: A rock or stone. A modern feminine form of Peter.
Pierah	Aboriginal	The moon.
Pierette	Greek	Greek: A rock or stone. A modern feminine form of Peter.
Pierina	Greek	Greek: A rock or stone. A modern feminine form of Peter.
Pierrette		A stone or rock. From the name Pierre.
Pilar	Aboriginal/Spanish	Aboriginal: A spear. Spanish: supportive, a pillar.
Piltti		An unusual Finnish name.
Piper	English	A pipe player.
Pippa		A lover of horses. The feminine form of Philip.
Pivari	Hindu	A wife of Sukha.

Pixie	Celtic/English	A fairy or sprite.
Piyali	Hindu	Tree.
Placida	Latin	Peaceful, serene. Feminine form of Placido.
Platona	Greek	Wise, broad-shouldered.
Polly		Bitter, as in a bitterly wanted child. Also - The star of the sea.
Pollyanna		A combination of Polly and Anna.
Poloma	Choctaw Indian	Bow.
Polona	Slovenian	
Pomona	Latin	Fertile, fruitful.
Pooja	Hindu	Prayer.
Poonam	Hindu	
Poppy	Old English	A flower name.
Portia	Latin	An offering. The name of the heroine in Shakespeare's The Merchant of Venice.
Posy	English	A bunch of flowers. Also a nickname for Josephine.
Prabha	Hindu	Lustrous.
Prabhati	Hindu	Morning.
Prachi	Hindu	
Pradeepta	Hindu	Glowing.
Pragati	Hindu	Progress.
Pragya	Hindu	Wisdom.
Prama	Hindu	Knowing truth.
Pramada	Hindu	Woman.
Pranati	Hindu	Prayer.
Prapti	Hindu	Gain.
Prasert	Thai	
Prashanti	Hindu	Peace.
Pratiksha	Hindu	
Pratima	Hindu	Image.
Preeti	Hindu	Love.
Preita	Finnish	Most loving one.
Prema	Sanskrit	Love, affection.
Premila	Hindu	
Prerana	Hindu	
Preyasi	Hindu	Beloved.
Prima	Latin	The firstborn.

Primavera	Spanish	Springtime, a child of the spring.
Primrose	Latin	The first rose. A flower name.
Primula		A flower name. See Primrose.
Prioska	Hungarian	The blushing one.
Priscilla	Latin	From a Roman family name.
Prisha	Hindu	
Prita		
Priti	Hindu	Satisfaction, renowned wife of Pulastya/Sukha.
Pritika	Hindu	Beloved.
Priya	Sanskrit	Beloved.
Priyanka	Hindu	
Prospera	Latin	Favorable.
Prudence	Latin	Provident, showing careful foresight.
Prue		Provident, showing careful foresight.
Prunella	Latin	A little plum.
Psyche	Greek	Of the soul or mind.
Ptolema	Greek	
Pulkita	Hindu	
Pundari	Hindu	
Punita	Hindu	
Purnima	Sanskrit	The night of the full moon.
Purva	Hindu	
Purvaja	Hindu	elder sister
Purvi	Hindu	
Pusti	Hindu	Nourishment, a form of the Devi, wife of Ganapati.
Pyrena	Greek	The fiery one.
Pythia	Greek	A prophet.
Qadira	Arabic	Powerful.
Qamra	Arabic	Moon.
Queena	Old English	A woman.
Queenie		Queen or female companion.
Quella	English	To pacify.
Quenby	Scandinavian	Womanly.
Quentin	Latin	The fifth, as in the fifth-born child.
Querida	Spanish	The beloved one.
Questa	French	The searcher.

Quincy	Latin/French	The fifth, as in fifth child.
Quinn	Irish Gaelic	Wise and intelligent.
Quinta	Latin	The fifth, as in fifth child. Also see Quentin.
Quintessa	Latin	Essence.
Quintina	Latin	Fifth.
Quirita	Latin	A citizen.
Quiterie	French	Tranquil.
Quoba	Latin	A citizen.
Quorra	Italian	Heart.
Rabi	Arabic	The harvest, or the spring.
Rach	African	Frog.
Rachael		A ewe.
Rachel	Hebrew	A ewe. The wife of Jacob and mother of Joseph in the Bible.
Rachelle		A ewe.
Rachna	Hindu	
Rada	Slavonic	Glad.
Radella	Old English	An elfin adviser.
Radha	Sanskrit	Success. The name of a Hindu goddess.
Radhika	Hindu	A form of the Devi, 5th Sakti, wife of Krishna.
Radinka	Slavonic	Joyful, active.
Radmilla	Slavonic	A worker for the people.
Rae	English	A doe.
Raeka	Spanish	Beautiful, unique.
Raelene	Australian	A modern invented name.
Raelin	Celtic	
Rafaela		The divine healer, or healed by God. Feminine form of Raphael.
Rafaella		
Raghnailt	Irish Gaelic	A ewe.
Ragini	Hindu	
Ragnhild	Norse	One who is wise in battle.
Rahab	Hebrew	
Rahel	Hebrew	A ewe.
Rai	Japanese	Trust.
Raimy	Raimee	
Rain	Latin	Ruler.
Rainbow	Old English	An array of bright colors.

Raine	Old German	Advice, decision.
Raisa	Russian from Greek	Adaptable.
Raissa	Old French	The believer.
Raizel	Hebrew	Rose.
Raja	Arabic	The hopeful one.
Rajani	Sanskrit	Dark, of the night.
Rajni	Hindu	
Rakel	Scandinavian	A ewe.
Rakhi	Hindu	
Raksha	Hindu	
Ramla	Swahili	One who predicts the future.
Ramona	Spanish	A wise protector. The feminine form of Ramon or Raymond.
Ramya	Hindu	Elegant, beautiful.
Rana	Arabic	Beautiful to gaze upon. Also see Rani.
Randa		The admired one.
Randie		A wolf-like shield or the admired one.
Randy		A wolf-like shield or the admired one.
Rane		Queen.
Ranee		Queen.
Rangi	Maori/Polynesian	Heaven or the sky.
Rani	Sanskrit	A queen.
Ranjana	Hindu	
Ranjita	Hindu	
Raphaela	Hebrew	The divine healer, or healed by God. Feminine form of Raphael.
Raphaella	Hebrew	Healed by God.
Raquel	Spanish	A ewe. The wife of Jacob and mother of Joseph in the Bible.
Raquelle		A ewe. The wife of Jacob and mother of Joseph in the Bible.
Rashida	Arabic	Righteous.
Rasika	Hindu	
Rasine	Polish	A rose.
Rasna	Hindu	
Rata	Aboriginal/Polynesian	Aboriginal: A plant. Polynesian: The name of a great chief.
Rati	Sanskrit	Love.

Rawnie	Gypsy	Lady.
Ray	Old French	A stream or a king.
Rayelle		
Raylene	Raylina	
Rayma		A wise protector. The feminine form of Ramon or Raymond.
Rayna	Polish/Czech	A queen.
Raziya	African	Agreeable.
Reanna		A nymph, or a queen.
Reba		A heifer or a knotted cord.
Rebecca	Hebrew	A heifer or a knotted cord. The wife of Isaac in the Bible.
Rebekah	Hebrew	A heifer or a knotted cord. The wife of Isaac in the Bible.
Rebel	Latin	The rebellious one.
Reena	Hindu	
Regan	Irish Gaelic	The descendant of a king.
Regina	Latin	The descendant of a king.
Rei	Japanese	Gratitude.
Reidun	Norwegian	Nest, lovely.
Reiko	Japanese	Gratitude.
Reina	Polish/Czech	A queen.
Reine	French	A queen.
Reka	Maori	Sweet.
Rekha	Hindu	Straight line.
Reman	Hindu	
Ren	Japanese	Water lily.
Rena	Hebrew	A joyous song.
Renata	Latin	Reborn.
Rene	Latin	Reborn.
Renee	French	Reborn.
Renita	Latin	A rebel.
Renny	Irish Gaelic	Small but powerful.
Renuka	Hindu	
Rere	Maori	A waterfall.
Reseda	Latin	A mignonette flower.
Reshma	Hindu	silky
Reva	Latin	Renewed strength.
Revati	Hindu	Wife of Balarama.
Revelation	Latin	To reveal.

Rewa	Polynesian	Slender.
Rexana	Latin	Regally graceful.
Rhea	Greek	A stream, or a mother.
Rhiamon	Welsh	Witch.
Rhiannon	Welsh	A nymph, or a queen.
Rhoda	Greek	A rose, or a woman from the island of Rhodes.
Rhodanthe	Greek	A rose.
Rhona		Variation of Rona. The name of a Scottish Island.
Rhonda	Welsh	After the name of a valley.
Rhonwen	Welsh	A white lance, or white hair.
Rhoswen	Gaelic	White rose.
Ria	Spanish	Of the river.
Riane	Gaelic	Little king.
Rianna		Sweet basil, virtuous.
Rianne		God is gracious.
Riannon		
Riba		A heifer or a knotted cord.
Ricarda		Brave and strong. Feminine form of Richard.
Richelle	Old German, Old English	Powerful ruler, brave one.
Rickena	Czech	
Riddhi	Hindu	Siddhi will follow.
Rieko	Japanese	Child of Rie.
Rihana	Arabic	Sweet basil.
Rikako	Japanese	Child of Rika.
Riley	Irish Gaelic/Old English	Irish Gaelic: Valiant. Old English: A Rye meadow.
Rilla	Teutonic	A stream.
Rima	Hindu	
Rina		A queen.
Rinako	Japanese	Child of Rina.
Rini	Japanese	Little bunny.
Rinzen	Tibetan/Sherpa	The holder of intellect.
Riona	Irish Gaelic	A queen, queen-like.
Risa	Latin	Laughter.
Risako	Japanese	Child of Risa.
Rishbha	Hindu	
Rishona	Hebrew	First.
Rita		A pearl.

Ritsuko	Japanese	Child of Ritsu.
Ritu	Hindu	
Riva	French from Latin	The shore or a river bank.
Rivka	Hebrew	A heifer or a knotted cord.
Rizpah	Greek	Hope.
Roanna	Latin	Gracious. Also derived from other names such as Rose and Anna.
Robalyn		Derived from Robin and Lynn.
Robbin		A small bird.
Roberta	Germanic/Old English	Bright fame, famous. Feminine form of Robert.
Robin	English	A small bird.
Robyn	English	A small bird.
Rochelle	French	A small rock. Also from La Rochelle, a French fishing port.
Roden	Old English	From the valley of the reeds.
Roderica	Teutonic	A famous ruler. Feminine form of Roderick.
Rohana	Sanskrit	Sandalwood.
Rohini	Hindu	
Rois	Irish Gaelic	The flower Rose (Rosa). Also: From the word for a horse.
Roisin	Irish Gaelic	The flower Rose (Rosa). Also: From the word for a horse.
Rolanda	Teutonic	From the famed land. Feminine form of Roland.
Roma	Latin	From Rome.
Romaine	Latin	A citizen of Rome. Feminine form of Roman.
Romana	Italian	From Rome.
Romilda	Teutonic	A glorious warrior maiden.
Romy	German	Dew of the sea, and the name of a fragrant herb. Also a combination of Rose and Mary.
Rona	Scottish	The name of an island.
Ronalda	Old Norse	Powerful. Also a feminine form of Ronald.
Ronan	Irish Gaelic	Little seal.
Ronda		Grand.
Ronni		A true likeness or image.
Ronnie		A true likeness or image.
Ronny		A true likeness or image.

Rory	Irish Gaelic	The red king.
Ros	Old German/Latin	Old German: From the word for a horse. Latin: Beautiful rose.
Rosa	Italian and Spanish	The flower Rose (Rosa). Also: From the word for a horse.
Rosabelle	Latin	A beautiful rose. Also derived from Rose and Belle.
Rosalba	Italian	A white rose.
Rosaleen	Irish	From the word for a horse. Also: Beautiful Rose.
Rosalia	Latin	Derived from Rose. Also the name of a 12th-century saint. Latin: The flower Rose (Rosa). Old German: From the word for a horse.
Rosalind	Old German/Latin	Old German: From the word for a horse. Latin: Beautiful Rose. Shakespeare's heroine in As You Like It.
Rosaline	Irish	From the word for a horse. Also: Beautiful Rose.
Rosalyn		From the word for a horse. Also: Beautiful Rose.
Rosamond	Old German/Latin	Old German: From the word for a horse. Latin: A pure rose, or the rose of the world.
Rosamunde		Wild roses.
Rosanna		A name derived from Rose and Anna. Rose - The flower Rose (Rosa). Also:From the word for a horse. Anna - Grace, or favored by God.
Rosanne	Latin	Gracious rose.
Rosario	Spanish	A rosary.
Rose	Latin/Old German	The flower Rose (Rosa). Also: From the word for a horse.
Roseanne		A name derived from Rose and Anna.
Roselani	Hawaiian	Heavenly rose.
Roselle		A combination of Rose and Elle.
Rosemary	Latin	Dew of the sea, and the name of a fragrant herb.
Rosen	Cornish	The flower Rose (Rosa). Also: From the word for a horse.
Rosenwyn	Cornish	A fair rose.

Rosetta	Italian	The flower Rose (Rosa). Also: From the word for a horse.
Rosevear	Cornish	From the moorland.
Roshan	Persian	Splendid, one who emanates light.
Rosheen	Irish Gaelic	The flower Rose (Rosa). Also: From the word for a horse.
Roshni	Hindu	Light.
Rosie	Latin/Old German	Latin: The flower Rose (Rosa). Old German: From the word for a horse.
Rosine		Little rose.
Rosita	Spanish	The flower Rose (Rosa). Also: From the word for a horse.
Roslyn	Old German/Latin	Old German: From the word for a horse. Latin: Beautiful rose.
Rossa	Scottish Gaelic	Woody meadow. Feminine form of Ross.
Rosy	Latin/Old German	Latin: The flower Rose (Rosa). Old German: From the word for a horse.
Rowan	Irish Gaelic	Little red-haired one.
Rowena	Celtic/Old English	Celtic: The white-haired one. Old English: A well-known friend.
Roxana	Persian	Dawn. The name of the wife of Alexander the Great.
Roxanne	Persian	Brilliant one.
Royale	Old French	The regal one. Feminine form of Roy.
Roz	Old German/Latin	Old German: From the word for a horse. Latin: Beautiful rose.
Roza	Polish	Rose.
Rozanne		A name derived from Rose and Anna.
Rozella		A combination of Rose and Elle.
Rozelle		A combination of Rose and Elle.
Ruby	Latin	Red, and the name of a precious stone.
Ruchi	Hindu	
Ruchika	Hindu	
Ruchira	Hindu	
Rudelle	Teutonic	The famous one.
Rudrani	Hindu	A wife of Shiva.

Rue	Old English from Greek	The name of an aromatic medicinal plant.
Ruella		A combination of Ruth and Ella.
Rufina	Latin	Red-haired. The feminine form of Rufus.
Rukmini	Sanskrit	The wife of Lord Krishna. Often used in Indonesia.
Rula	Latin	A ruler.
Rumer	English	A gipsy.
Rumiko	Japanese	Child of Rumi.
Runa	Old Norse	Secret love.
Rupa	Hindu	
Rupal	Hindu	
Rupali	Hindu	
Ruperta	German	Bright fame, famous. Feminine form of Robert. Also see Robin.
Ruri	Japanese	An emerald.
Ruth	Hebrew	Beautiful and compassionate. A biblical name.
Ryann	Irish Gaelic	A little king.
Ryba	Czech	Fish.
Ryesen	English	Rye.
Ryoko	Japanese	Child of Ryo.
Saba	Greek	Woman of Sheba.
Sabah	Arabic	The morning.
Sabella		A form of Elizabeth, meaning consecrated to God.
Sabelle		A form of Elizabeth, meaning consecrated to God.
Sabia	Irish	The sweet one.
Sabiha		
Sabina	Latin	Related to the Sabines.
Sabine	Latin	The Sabines were a tribe living in central Italy during the time of the establishment of Rome. The Romans kidnapped the Sabine women to provide brides for the citizens of Rome.
Sabira	Arabic	The patient one.
Sabirah	Arabic	Patient.
Sabra	Hebrew	A thorny cactus, or to rest.
Sabrina	Celtic	A legendary character.

Sacha	French	The defender, or helper of mankind.
Sachi	Japanese	Joy.
Sachiko	Japanese	Bliss, child of Sachi.
Sadb	Gaelic	
Sade	Nigerian	Honor confers a crown.
Sadhana	Hindu	
Sadie		A princess. The wife of Abraham and mother of Isaac in the Bible.
Sadira	Persian	A lotus.
Saeko	Japanese	Child of Sae.
Safak	Turkish	
Saffi	Danish	Form of Sophie. Wisdom.
Saffron	Arabic	From the name of the spice.
Safia	Arabic	The confidante, or pure one.
Safiya	African	Pure.
Sagara	Hindu	Ocean.
Sage	Old French	Wise.
Sahana	Hindu	
Sahar	Arabic	Dawn.
Saheli	Hindu	Friend.
Sahiba	Hindu	Lady.
Sahila	Hindu	Guide.
Saida	Arabic	Fortunate one.
Saidah	African	Happy, fortunate.
Sajili	Hindu	Decorated.
Sajni	Hindu	Beloved.
Sakari	Native American	Sweet.
Sakiko	Japanese	Child of Saki.
Sakinah	Arabic	God-inspired peace-of-mind, tranquility.
Sakti	Hindu	Energy, goodness.
Sakuko	Japanese	Child of Saku.
Sakura	Japanese	Cherry blossom.
Sakurako	Japanese	Child of Sakura.
Salal	English	A plant.
Salihah	African	Correct.
Salima	Arabic	Safe, secure.
Salimah	Arabic	Safe, healthy.
Salina	Latin	Solemn.

Sally		A princess. The wife of Abraham and mother of Isaac in the Bible.
Saloma	Hebrew	Peace. A biblical name.
Salome	Hebrew	Peace. A biblical name.
Saloni	Hindu	Dear, beautiful.
Salvia	Latin	A plant name.
Salwa	Arabic	Solace, comfort.
Sam		She who listens also an achievement.
Samantha	Aramaic	She who listens.
Samara	Hebrew	Guarded by God.
Samicah	Hebrew	
Samiksha	Hindu	
Samirah	Arabic	Entertaining companion.
Samma	Arabic	Sky.
Sammi		She who listens.
Sammie		She who listens also an achievement.
Sammy		She who listens also an achievement.
Sampriti	Hindu	Attachment.
Samta	Hindu	
Samuela	Hebrew	Asked of God. The feminine form of Samuel.
Samularia		Sweet one forever.
Samye		
Sana	Arabic	The radiant one.
Sanako	Japanese	Child of Sana.
Sanchay	Hindu	Collection.
Sancia	Latin	Sacred.
Sandi		The defender, or helper of mankind.
Sandia	Spanish	Watermelon.
Sandie	Greek	The protector and helper of mankind.
Sandra		The defender, or helper of mankind.
Sandrine	Greek	The defender, or helper of mankind.
Sandy	Greek	The defender, or helper of mankind.
Sandya	Hindu	Sunset time, name of a God.
Sangita	Hindu	Musical.

Sangmu	Tibetan/Sherpa	The kind-hearted one.
Sanjna	Hindu	Wife of the Sun.
Sanjula	Hindu	Beautiful.
Sanrevelle	Portuguese	
Sanyogita	Hindu	
Sanyukta	Hindu	
Sapna	Hindu	Dream.
Sapphira	Greek	Deep blue. A gemstone name.
Sapphire	Greek	Deep blue. A gemstone name.
Sara		A princess. The wife of Abraham and mother of Isaac in the Bible.
Sarah	Hebrew	A princess. The wife of Abraham and mother of Isaac in the Bible.
Sarai	Hebrew	Quarrelsome.
Saraid	Celtic	Excellent.
Sarala	Sanskrit	Honest.
Sarasvati	Hindu	A Goddess.
Saravati	Hindu	
Sarea	Hebrew	Name of an angel.
Saree	Arabic	Most noble.
Saria	Hebrew	A princess. The wife of Abraham and mother of Isaac in the Bible.
Sariah	Hebrew	Hebrew expression meaning Princess of the Lord.
Sarika	Hindu	Thrush.
Sarisha	Sanskrit	Charming.
Sarita	Hindu	Stream, river.
Sarmistha	Hindu	A daughter of Vrsaparvan.
Saroja	Sanskrit	Born in a lake.
Saru	Hindu	
Saryu	Hindu	A river in Ramayana
Sasha	Russian	The protector and helper of mankind.
Sashenka	Russian	Defender and helper of mankind.
Sashi	Hindu	
Saskia	Dutch	A Saxon.
Sasthi	Hindu	
Satinka	Native American	Magic dancer.
Satoko	Japanese	Child of Sato.
Satyavati		

Saumya	Hindu	
Saundarya	Hindu	
Savanna	Spanish	From the Grasslands or open plains.
Savarna	Hindu	Daughter of the ocean.
Savina	Russian	A Sabine woman (from central Italy).
Savita	Hindu	Sun.
Savitri	Hindu	A form of the Devi, 4th Sakti.
Sawsan	Arabic	A lily of the valley.
Saxon	Old English	Of the Saxons, or people of the sword.
Saxona	Teutonic	A Saxon.
Sayoko	Japanese	Child of Sayo.
Scarlet		Flaming red.
Scarlett	Old French	A color name, Made famous by the heroine in Margaret Mitchell's Gone With the Wind.
Schmetterling	German	Butterfly.
Schuyler	Dutch	Shield, scholar.
Scota	Latin	An Irish woman.
Seanna	Celtic	God's grace.
Searlait	French	Small and wise.
Season	Latin	The time of sowing.
Sebastiana	Latin	A woman from Sebasta. The feminine form of Sebastian.
Sebastianne	Latin	Revered one.
Secunda	Latin	The second child.
Seema	Greek, Hindu	Symbol.
Sefika	Turkish	
Seirian	Welsh	Sparkling.
Seiriol	Welsh	The bright one.
Sela	Hebrew	A rock.
Selda		The grey battle heroine.
Selena	Greek	The goddess of the moon.
Selene	Greek	The goddess of the moon.
Selia		The blind one, or the sixth. The feminine form of Cecil.
Selima		Brings comfort, peace.
Selina		Lunar glow.
Selma		A divine helmet.

Semele	Greek	A figure from Greek mythology.
Semine	Danish	Goddess of sun, moon and stars.
Semra	Turkish	
Senga	Scottish Gaelic	The slender one.
Senta	Old German	Assistant.
Seonaid	Scottish Gaelic	God is gracious.
Septima	Latin	The seventh born.
Serafina		Heavenly, winged angel.
Seraphina	Hebrew	The ardent burning one. The Seraphim are an order of angels in the Bible.
Serena	Latin	Calm, serene.
Serendipity		Good fortune.
Serenity		Peaceful disposition.
Serica	Latin	The silken one.
Serilda	Teutonic	The armored battle maiden.
Sesha	Hindu	Serpent who symbolizes time.
Sevati	Hindu	White rose.
Seve	Breton	
Severina	Latin	The stem or severe one.
Sevilla	Spanish	The name of a city.
Sevita	Hindu	Beloved.
Sexburth	Anglo-Saxon	
Sezen	Turkish	
Shahira	Arabic	Famous.
Shahnaz	Persian	The pride of the emperor.
Shaila	Hindu	
Shailaja	Hindu	
Shaili	Hindu	Style.
Shaina	Hebrew	Beautiful.
Shaine	Hebrew	beautiful
Shakira	Arabic	Thankful.
Shako	Native American	Mint.
Shakti	Sanskrit	The powerful one.
Shakuntala	Sanskrit	A bird.
Shalini	Hindu	
Shamita	Hindu	Peacemaker.
Shammara	Arabic	he girded his loins
Shana		God is gracious.
Shanata	Hindu	Peaceful.

Shane	Irish Gaelic	From Irish Gaelic a Variation of Sean (John), and so a form of Jane.
Shanelle		The name of a famous perfume.
Shanessa	Irish	God is gracious.
Shani	Swahili	Wonderful. Also a form of Sian.
Shanna		Small and wise.
Shannah	Irish Gaelic	From an old surname.
Shannelle	French	Channel.
Shannon	Irish	From the name of a river in Ireland.
Shantah	Hindu	Peace, name of a God.
Shantal		From a family name meaning stone or boulder. The name has also come to mean a little singer.
Shantay	French	Enchanted.
Shantel		From a family name meaning stone or boulder. The name has also come to mean a little singer.
Shantell		Rocky area.
Shantelle		From a family name meaning stone or boulder. The name has also come to mean a little singer.
Shanti	Sanskrit	The tranquil one.
Shantina		Warrior princess.
Sharay		
Sharda	Hindu	
Sharee		A princess.
Shari		A princess.
Sharleen		A free person.
Sharlene		A free person.
Sharman		Delightful.
Sharmila	Sanskrit	The protected one.
Sharmistha	Hindu	
Sharney		A flat plain.
Sharni		A flat plain.
Sharnie		A flat plain.
Sharon	Hebrew	A flat plain. After a biblical location.
Sharseia		
Shashi	Hindu	The moon, moonbeam.
Shasmecka	African	princess
Shauna		God is gracious.

Shaunna		God is gracious.
Shavonne	Irish Gaelic	Form of Jane and Judith. Jane - God is gracious. Judith - A woman from Judea.
Shawmbria		
Shawn	Irish Gaelic	God is gracious.
Shawna		God is gracious.
Shawnnessy	Irish, Native American	
Shay	Irish Gaelic	The stately one.
Shayla	Celtic	Fairy palace.
Shayna	Jewish	Beautiful.
Shayndel	Yiddish	Beautiful.
Sheba	Greek	A woman of Sheba, an ancient Arabian country.
Sheela	Sanskrit	Of good character.
Sheena	Scottish Gaelic	God is gracious.
Sheetal	Hindu	Cool.
Sheila		The blind one, or the sixth. Irish form of Cecilia.
Shela	Celtic	Musical.
Shelah	Hebrew	Request.
Shelby	Old English	The dweller at the ledge estate and a sheltered town.
Shelley	Old English	From the wood, or the meadow's edge.
Shelton	Old English	From the place on the ledge.
Sher	Sanskrit	The beloved one or a Lion.
Sheree		The beloved one.
Sheridan	Irish Gaelic	The wild one.
Sherri		The beloved one.
Sherrie		The beloved one.
Sherry		The beloved one.
Shevaun	Irish Gaelic	Form of Jane and Judith. Jane - God is gracious. Judith - A woman from Judea.
Shian		
Shiela		Blind.
Shifra	Hebrew	Beauty and grace. A biblical name.
Shika	Japanese	Deer.
Shikha	Hindu	
Shin	Korean	Belief.

Shina	Japanese	Virtue, good.
Shira	Hebrew	My song.
Shirin	Persian	Charming.
Shirley	Old English	From the bright meadow. Originally a boy's name.
Shirlyn		Bright meadow.
Shivani	Hindu	
Shivaun	Irish Gaelic	Form of Jane and Judith. Jane - God is gracious. Judith - A woman from Judea.
Shobha	Hindu	
Shobhana	Sanskrit	The beautiful one.
Shobhna	Hindu	
Shobi	Hebrew	Glorious.
Shoko	Japanese	Child of Sho.
Shona	Scottish Gaelic	God is gracious.
Shoshana	Hebrew	A Lily, or a Rose.
Shoshanah	Hebrew	Rose.
Shoshannah	Hebrew	Rose.
Shradhdha	Hindu	
Shreya	Hindu	Auspicious.
Shri	Hindu	Lustre, shine.
Shridevi	Hindu	
Shrijani	Hindu	Creative.
Shruti	Hindu	Hearing.
Shubha	Hindu	
Shulamit	Hebrew	Peacefulness.
Shylah	Celtic	Loyal to God, strong.
Shysie	Native American	Silent little one.
Sian	Welsh	God is gracious.
Sibel	Turkish	
Sibley	Greek	Prophetess.
Sibongile	African	Thanks.
Sibyl		The prophetess. From Greek mythology.
Siddhi	Hindu	Then you must have a Riddhi.
Sidonia		To entice.
Sidonie	Latin	A woman from Sidon, in modern-day Lebanon.
Sidra	Latin	Of the stars.
Siena	Italian	A city in Tuscany.

Sienna	Italian	Reddish brown.
Sierra	Latin	From the mountains.
Signe	Swedish	A sign, victorious.
Signild	Scandinavian	
Signy	Old Norse	A new victory.
Sigourney	Old Norse	The conqueror.
Sigrid	Old Norse	A beautiful victory.
Sigrun	Old Norse	A secret victory.
Siham	Arabic	Arrows.
Sile	Irish Gaelic	The blind one, or the sixth. The feminine form of Cecil.
Sileas	Scottish Gaelic	The blind one, or the sixth. The feminine form of Cecil.
Silei	Samoan	
Silke	German	The blind one, or the sixth. .
Silva		From the forest.
Silvana	Italian	From the forest.
Silver	Old English	The fair or silvery one.
Silvestra	Latin	Of the woods.
Silvia	Latin	From the forest.
Silvie		From the forest.
Simba	Swahili	Lion.
Simone	Hebrew	The listener. The feminine form of Simon.
Simoni	Hindu	Obedient.
Simran	Hindu	God's Gift
Sindy		A maiden of the cinders or ashes.
Sine	Gaelic	God's gracious gift.
Sinead	Irish Gaelic	God is gracious.
Siobhan	Irish Gaelic	Form of Jane and Judith. Jane - God is gracious. Judith - A woman from Judea.
Sioned	Welsh	God is gracious.
Siran	Armenian	Alluring.
Sirena	Greek	A sea nymph. In mythology, the Sirens lured mariners to their death through seductive singing.
Siri		A beautiful victory.
Sirikit	Thai	The name of a queen.
Sirisha	Hindu	
Siroun	Armenian	Lovely.

Sissey		The blind one, or the sixth.
Sissie		The blind one, or the sixth.
Sissy		The blind one, or the sixth.
Sita	Sanskrit	A furrow. The Hindu goddess of the harvest.
Sitara	Sanskrit	Morning star.
Sitembile	African	Trust.
Siv	Norwegian	Kinship, wife of Thor.
Skye	Scottish	An island in the Inner Hebrides.
Skyla	English	Sky, sheltering.
Skylar	English	Eternal life, strength, love and beauty.
Smita	Hindu	Smiling.
Smridhi	Hindu	
Smriti	Hindu	Recollection, a form of the Devi.
Sneh	Hindu	
Sneha	Hindu	
Snigdha	Hindu	
Snofrid	Scandinavian	
Sobha	Hindu	
Sofia	Norwegian/Swedish	Wisdom.
Sofie	Danish/Dutch	Wisdom.
Solace	Latin	Comfort.
Solana	Spanish	The sun.
Solange	Latin	The solemn one. A French name.
Soledad	Spanish	Good health.
Soleil	French	Sun.
Solita	Latin	Alone.
Solosolo	Samoan	Dry.
Solveig	Old Norse	From the strong house. The heroine of Henrik Ibsen's Peer Gynt, and generally a Norwegian name.
Somatra	Hindu	Excelling the moon.
Sona	Hindu	Gold.
Sonakshi	Hindu	Golden eye.
Sonal	Hindu	Golden.
Sonam	Tibetan/Sherpa	The fortunate one.
Sondra		The defender, or helper of mankind. From the name Alexandra.
Sonia		Wisdom.

Sonika	Hindu	Golden.
Sonnenschein	German	Sunshine.
Sonya	Russian	Wisdom.
Soo	Korean	Along life.
Sophia	Greek	Wisdom.
Sophie	Greek	Wisdom.
Sophronia	Greek	Sensible.
Sorano	Japanese	Of the sky.
Soraya	Farsi	Princess.
Sorcha	Gaelic	Brightness.
Sorilbran		Smart.
Sorrel	Old French	Bitter. From the name of the tree.
Sparrow	English	A bird.
Spica	Latin	Name of a star.
Spring	English	Spring season.
Sraddha	Hindu	Faith, a wife of Shiva.
Srilata	Hindu	
Sripada	Hindu	
Srishti	Hindu	
Sruti	Hindu	
Stacey		She who will rise again. From the name Anastasia and Eustacia.
Stacia		Resurrection.
Stacy	Latin	Prosperous or resurrection.
Star	English	A star. Also see Stella.
Starr	Old English	A star.
Stefania	Greek	Crown.
Stefanie		A garland or crown.
Steffi	German	A garland or crown.
Steffie		A garland or crown.
Stella	Latin	A star. Also see Estelle, Esther and Star.
Stephanie	Greek	A garland or crown.
Stephenie		A garland or crown.
Stesha	Greek	Crowned one.
Stina		A follower of Christ, a Christian.
Stockard	English	From the yard of tree stumps.
Storm	Old English	A tempest.
Stormy		Impetuous nature.
Subhadra	Hindu	A wife of Arjuna.

Subhaga	Hindu	A fortunate person.
Subhangi	Hindu	
Subhuja	Hindu	Auspicious.
Suchi	Hindu	
Suchitra	Hindu	
Sudevi	Hindu	Wife of Krishna.
Sudha	Hindu	
Sue		A lily.
Suellen		From Susan and Ellen. Susan - A Lily. Ellen - The light of the sun.
Sujata	Sanskrit	Of noble birth.
Sujatmi	Indonesian	A popular girl's name.
Sukanya	Hindu	
Suki		A lily.
Suksma	Hindu	
Sukutai	African	Hug.
Sula	Icelandic	The sun.
Sulema		Peace.
Sultana	Arabic	A queen or empress.
Suma	Egyptian, Japanese	To ask.
Sumalee	Thai	A beautiful flower.
Sumanna	Hindu	
Sumati	Hindu	
Sumehra	Arabic	Beautiful face.
Sumey	Asian	flower
Sumi	Japanese	The refined one.
Sumitra	Hindu	
Summer	Old English	After the season.
Sun	Chinese/Korean	Chinese: Bending, or decreasing. Korean: Goodness.
Sundeep	Hindu	
Sunee	Thai	Good.
Sunita	Sanskrit	Of good conduct.
Suniti	Hindu	
Sunniva	Old English	The gift of the sun.
Sunny	English	Bright, cheerful.
Suparna	Hindu	Leafy.
Suprabha	Hindu	Radiant.
Supriti	Hindu	

Supriya	Hindu	Su means good and Priya means loved one.
Surabhi	Hindu	wish-yielding cow
Suravinda	Hindu	A beautiful Yaksa.
Surotama	Hindu	Auspicious.
Suruchi	Hindu	
Surupa	Hindu	
Susan	Hebrew	A Lily.
Susanna	Italian	A Lily.
Susannah	Hebrew	A Lily. The original, biblical, form of Susan. Also see Susan.
Susanne	German	A Lily.
Sushanti	Hindu	Peace.
Sushma	Hindu	
Sushmita	Hindu	Smiling.
Susi		A Lily.
Susie		A Lily.
Susila	Hindu	Wife of Krishna, clever in amorous sciences.
Susy		A Lily.
Suvarna	golden	
Suvrata	Hindu	A child of Daksa.
Suzanne	French	A Lily.
Suzette	French	A Lily.
Suzie		A Lily.
Suzy		A Lily. From the name Susan.
Svea	Swedish	A woman of Sweden.
Svetlana	Slavonic	Light. Generally a Russian name.
Swanhild	Teutonic	A swan of battle.
Swarupa	Hindu	Truth.
Swati	Hindu	
Sweta	Hindu	
Sybil	Greek	The prophetess. From Greek mythology.
Sydelle	Hebrew	Princess.
Sydnee		Derived from Saint Denys.
Sydney	Old English/Old French	Old English: From the riverside meadow. Old French: From St Denis. More often a boy's name.
Syeira	Gypsy	Princess.
Sylvia	Latin	From the forest.

Sylvie	French	From the forest. From the name Sylvia.
Syna	Greek	Together.
Syria	Aramaic	The name of a Middle Eastern country.
Syshe	Yiddish	Street.
Tabitha	Aramaic	A doe or gazelle. A biblical name.
Taborri	Native American	Voices that carry.
Taci	Zuni Indian	Washtub.
Tacincala	Native American	Deer.
Tacita	Latin	Silent or peaceful.
Tadako	Japanese	Child of Tada.
Tadi	Omaha Indian	Wind.
Tahira	Arabic	Pure and virtuous.
Tahirah	Arabic	Chaste, pure.
Tahnee		Silver-haired.
Tahnia		Silver-haired.
Tailynn	unknown	
Taima	Native American	Crash of thunder.
Tainn	Native American	New moon.
Taipa	Miwok Indian	To spread wings.
Tajsa	princess	
Taka	Japanese	Tall, or honorable.
Takako	Japanese	Child of Taka
Takara	Japanese	A treasure.
Takiyah	North African	Pious, righteous.
Tala	Native American	Stalking wolf.
Talasi	Hopi Indian	Corn-tassel flower.
Tale	African	Green.
Taleen	Armenian	
Talia	Various	Aboriginal: Near water. Greek: Flourishing. Hebrew: Dew. Russian: Born at Christmas. From the name Natalya.
Talitha	Aramaic	A little girl or maiden. A biblical name.
Tallara	Aboriginal	Rain.
Tallulah	Native American	Running water.
Talon		
Talulla	Irish Gaelic	A prosperous lady.
Talwyn	Cornish	A fair brow.

Talya	Russian	Born at Christmas. From the name Natalya.
Tam	Scottish	A twin or heart.
Tama	Japanese/Polynesian	Japanese: A jewel. Polynesian: A boy or son.
Tamah		A jewel. From the name Tama.
Tamali	Hindu	
Tamara	Hebrew	A palm tree. A popular name in Germany and Russia.
Tamasine		Twin.
Tamatha		A palm tree. A popular name in Germany and Russia.
Tambrey		Immortal.
Tamera	Hebrew	A spice or palm tree.
Tamiko	Japanese	child of Tami
Tammi		A palm tree.
Tammie		A palm tree.
Tammy		A palm tree.
Tamora		From Shakespeare's play Titus Andronicus.
Tamsin	Cornish	A free person.
Tamsyn	Native American	
Tanaka	Japanese	Dweller.
Tanasha		Strong willed, persistent.
Tani	Japanese	From the valley.
Tania		Silver-haired.
Tansy	Greek	Immortal. A flower name.
Tanu	Hindu	
Tanuja	Hindu	
Tanushi	Hindu	
Tanvi	Hindu	
Tanya	Russian	Silver-haired.
Tao	Chinese	Long life.
Tapanga	African, Hebrew	Sweet, unpredictable.
Tapi	Hindu	
Tapti	Hindu	
Tara	Irish Gaelic/Sanskrit	Irish Gaelic: A rocky hill, from the ancient home of Ireland's kings. Sanskrit: A star. The name of a Buddhist goddess.
Tarana	Aboriginal	A large waterhole.
Taranga	Polynesian	A figure from legend.

Tarra	Aboriginal	A creek.
Tarsha	Native American	
Taryn		The name of a county in Northern Ireland. Feminine form of Tyrone.
Tasha		Born at Christmas.
Tashi	Tibetan/Sherpa	Prosperity.
Tasmine		Twin.
Tathra	Aboriginal	Beautiful country.
Tatum	Old English	From Tate's homestead.
Tatya	Aboriginal	
Tatyana	Latin	Silver-haired.
Tavia		The eighth.
Tawnie	English	Little one, yellowish-brown.
Tawny	Old French	With yellowish-brown hair.
Tayce	French	Silence.
Tayen	Native American	New moon.
Taylar	Old French	To cut.
Taylor	Old French	A tailor.
Teagan		
Teal	English	A water bird.
Tean	Cornish	One of the Isles of Scilly.
Tegan	Welsh	Of doe-like beauty.
Tegen	Cornish	A pretty little thing.
Tegwen	Welsh	Beautiful and blessed.
Tehya	Native American	Precious.
Tejal	Hindu	
Teji	Hindu	
Tekla	Greek	Divine fame.
Telma		A wish, or will.
Tema	Hebrew	Righteous, a palm tree.
Temina	Hebrew	Honest.
Temira	Hebrew	
Temperance	Latin	Moderate.
Tempest	Old French	Stormy.
Teneale		
Tenzin	Tibetan/Sherpa	Protector of Dharma.
Tenzing	Tibetan/Sherpa	Protector of Dharma.
Teofilia	Greek	Beloved by God.
Tereixa	Galician	

Terena	Latin	Earthly.
Terencia	Latin	Smooth and polished.
Terentia	Greek	guardian
Teresa	Greek	The harvester or reaper.
Terhi	Finish	
Teri	Greek	The harvester or reaper.
Terra	Latin	Earth
Terri	Greek	The harvester or reaper.
Terry	Greek/Latin	Greek: The harvester or reaper. Latin: Smooth and polished.
Terrylyn		
Tertia	Latin	The third child.
Terza		Pleasant.
Tesia	Polish	Loved by God.
Tess	Greek	The harvester or reaper.
Tessa	Greek	The harvester or reaper.
Tessie	Greek	The harvester or reaper.
Texcean	Tex	
Thaddea	Greek	Courageous.
Thais	Greek	The bond.
Thaisa		From Shakespeare's play Pericles.
Thalassa	Greek	From the sea.
Thalia		Born at Christmas.
Thana	Arabic	Gratitude.
Thanh	Vietnamese	Brilliant.
Thara	Arabic	Wealth.
Thea	Greek	A goddess.
Theano	Greek	A divine name.
Thecla	Greek	The glory of God.
Theda	Teutonic	Of the people. Also see Theodora.
Thelma	Greek	A wish, or will.
Theodora	Greek	The gift of God.
Theodosia	Greek	God-given.
Theone	Greek	Godly.
Theophania	Greek	A manifestation of God.
Theora	Greek	A thinker or watcher.
Thera	Greek	Wild. From the name of an island.
Theresa		The harvester or reaper.
Therese		The harvester or reaper.

Theresia	German	The harvester or reaper.
Thetis	Greek	Positive determined.
Thirza	Hebrew	Sweet natured, cypress tree.
Thisbe	Greek	Where the doves live.
Thistle	Old English	Thistle.
Thomasa	Greek	Twin.
Thomasina	Greek	A twin. The feminine form of Thomas.
Thora	Old Norse	Thunder.
Thorberta	Old Norse	The brilliance of Thor.
Thorborg	Scandinavian	
Thordis	Old Norse	The spirit of Thor.
Thurid	Scandinavian	
Thyra	Greek	A shield bearer.
Thyrrni	Scandinavian	
Tia	Spanish, Greek	Aunt, princess.
Tiara	Greek, Latin	Turban, flower name.
Tiberia	Latin	After the River Tiber.
Tiegan	Aztec	Little princess in the big valley.
Tienette	Greek	Crowned with laurel.
Tierney	Irish Gaelic	The descendant of a lord.
Tierra	Spanish	Earth, land.
Tiffany	Old English	A manifestation of God.
Tigerlily	Lily, Tiger	
Tilda		The mighty battle maiden.
Tillie		The mighty battle maiden.
Tilly		The mighty battle maiden.
Timandra		From Shakespeare's play Timon of Athens.
Timothea	Greek	Honoring God, or honored by God. The female form of Timothy.
Tina		
Tineka Jawana	African	
Tinka	Aboriginal	The day.
Tionne		
Tiponya	Miwok Indian	Owl poking the hatching egg.
Tirion	Welsh	Gentle.
Tirranna	Aboriginal	Running water.
Tirza	Hebrew	

Tirzah	Hebrew	Pleasant.
Titania	Greek	The great one. The name of the fairy queen in Shakespeare's A Midsummer Night's Dream.
Titian	Greek	Red-gold.
Tivona	Hebrew	Lover of nature.
Tizane	Hungarian	A gypsy.
Toakase	Tonga	Woman of the Sea.
Tobie	Hebrew	God is good.
Tobit	Hebrew	
Toinette		Beyond price, praiseworthy. The feminine form of Antony.
Tokiko	Japanese	Child of Toki.
Tola	Polish	Priceless.
Tolena	Toley	
Tomiko	Japanese	Child of Tomi.
Tona		
Toni		Priceless, praiseworthy.
Tonia		Priceless, praiseworthy.
Tonie		Priceless, praiseworthy.
Tonya		Priceless, praiseworthy.
Toora	Aboriginal	A woman.
Topaz	Greek	The name of a gemstone.
Tora	Japanese	A tiger.
Toral	Hindu	
Tori		Victory, the victorious one.
Torie		Victory, the victorious one.
Tory		Victory, the victorious one.
Tosia	Latin	Inestimable.
Totie		Gift of God.
Tottie		A free person
Totty		A free person.
Tourmaline	Singhalese	The name of a gemstone.
Tove	Hebrew	Good.
Toyo	Japanese	Plentiful.
Tracey	Old French	From a location.
Tracy	Old French	Brave.
Treasa	Irish/Gaelic	The harvester or reaper.
Tresa	Aragonic	
Tressa	Cornish	The third. Also see Teresa.

Treva	Celtic	Prudent.
Tricia		Noble, well-born. The feminine form of Patrick.
Trifine	Old French	
Trilby	Italian	Sings with trills.
Trilochana	Hindu	
Trina	Greek	Pure. Also a nickname from Catherine, Katherine and Katrina.
Trind	Swedish	Pure.
Trinidad	Spanish	After the Caribbean island.
Trinity	Latin	A trio or triad, as in the Holy Trinity.
Trish		Noble, well-born. The feminine form of Patrick.
Trisha		Noble, well-born. The feminine form of Patrick.
Trishna	Hindu	Thirst, a form of the Devi.
Trista	Latin	The melancholy one.
Tristana		Sad.
Tristessa		Bold.
Trix		The blessed one. She who brings joy. Beatrix was the name of a 4th-century saint.
Trixi		The blessed one.
Trixie		The blessed one.
Trixy		The blessed one.
Trude		From Gertrude.
Trudi		A spear maiden.
Trudie		A spear maiden.
Trudy		A spear maiden.
Trupti	Hindu	
Trusha	Hindu	
Tryne	Dutch	Pure.
Tryphena	Latin	Dainty.
Tuesday	Old English	Born on a Tuesday.
Tuhina	Hindu	
Tulasi	Hindu	A Devi.
Tulip	Turkish	A flower name.
Tullia	Irish Gaelic	Peaceful.
Tully	Celtic, Gaelic	A people, peaceful one.
Turquoise	Old French	A precious stone.
Turua	Polynesian	Beautiful.

Tusti	Hindu	Peace, happiness, a for of the Devi.
Tuti	Indonesian	An unusual girl's name.
Tuvia	Hebrew	God is good. The female form of Tobias.
Twyla	Old English	Woven with double thread.
Tyanne		Special one.
Tydfill	Welsh	
Tyler	Old English	A tiler or tile-maker.
Tyne		The name of an English river.
Uda	Teutonic	Prosperous, rich.
Udaya	Hindu	
Ujjwala	Hindu	
Ula	Celtic	A jewel of the sea.
Ulalia		The well-spoken one.
Ulani	Polynesian	Cheerful, light hearted.
Ulfhildr	Scandinavian	
Ulima	Arabic	Wise, learned.
Ulla	Aboriginal	A well.
Ulma	Latin	Of the Elm tree.
Ulrika	Old German, Old English	Wolf ruler.
Ulrike	Teutonic/Scandinavian	The ruler of all. The feminine form of Ulrich.
Ultima	Latin	The greatest, the most distant.
Ultreia	Galician	
Ulva	Teutonic	A she-wolf, brave.
Uma	Hebrew/Sanskrit	Hebrew: The nation. Sanskrit: Light, peace. Also the name of a goddess in Hindu mythology.
Umeko	Japanese	The child of the plum blossom.
Umina	Aboriginal	Sleep.
Una	Irish Gaelic/Latin	Irish Gaelic: A traditional name. Latin: One.
Unaiza	Arabic	
Undine		A water sprite.
Unice		Victorious.
Unity	English	Oneness. From the Latin 'unus', meaning one.
Unnati	Hindu	Progress.
Unni	Norse	Modest.
Urania	Greek	Heavenly.
Urbana	Latin	Courteous, belonging to the city.

Uriana	Greek	The unknown.
Urmila	Hindu	Wife of Lakshmana.
Ursala		Female bear.
Ursanne	Old French	
Ursell	Cornish	From the bottom of the hill.
Ursula	Latin	A female bear.
Urvasi	Hindu	Most beautiful of Apsaras.
Usagi	Japanese	Moon.
Uschi	German	A female bear.
Usha	Sanskrit	The dawn.
Ushma	Hindu	
Usoa	Basque	
Uta	German	Fortunate maid of battle.
Utah		The name of an American State.
Ute	Teutonic	Prosperity, fortunate, rich.
Utina	Native American	A woman of my country.
Uttara	Hindu	Mother of Pariksit.
Vada		
Valda	Teutonic	A ruler, a battle heroine.
Vaisakhi	Hindu	
Vaishali	Hindu	
Val		Strength, valor.
Vala	Teutonic	The chosen one.
Valarie		Strength, valor.
Valborg	Swedish	A powerful mountain.
Valda	Old Norse	Spirited warrior.
Valeda		Strong and healthy. Used in Russia and Eastern Europe.
Valencia		Bravery.
Valentina	Latin	Strong and healthy. Used in Russia and Eastern Europe.
Valentine	Latin	Strong, healthy. The name of a 3rd-century saint.
Valeria		Strength, valor.
Valerie	French	Strong.
Valeska	Polish	Glorious ruler.
Valgerdr	Scandinavian	
Valimai	Welsh	A mayflower.
Valisa		Wild one.
Vallerie		To be strong.

Valletta		The capital of Malta.
Valma		The chosen one.
Valonia	Latin	From the valley.
Valora	Latin	Brave.
Vanda	Aboriginal/Teutonic	Aboriginal: A sandhill. Teutonic: A Slavonic woman, or a wanderer.
Vandana	Hindu	
Vandita	Hindu	
Vanessa		A name invented by the 18th-century poet and writer Jonathan Swift.
Vania	Russian	God's gift.
Vanja	Scandinavian	The feminine form of Vanya, also a Russian Diminutive of Ivan. Eastern European form of John.
Vanjan	Hindu	
Vanka	Russian	Grace, or favored by God.
Vanni	Italian	Grace, or favored by God.
Vanora	Celtic	A white wave. A form of Guinevere.
Varanese	Italian	
Varda	Hebrew	A rose.
Varsha	Hindu	Rain.
Varuni	Hindu	A goddess.
Varvara	Russian	The foreigner or stranger. Russian form of Barbara.
Vasanta	Hindu	Spring.
Vasanti	Sanskrit	Spring.
Vasavi	Hindu	Daughter of the Pitrs.
Vashti	Persian	The beautiful one.
Vasiliki	Greek	Basil.
Vasudhara	Hindu	
Vasuki	Hindu	
Vasumati	Hindu	Apsara of unequaled splendor.
Veda	Sanskrit	Wisdom and knowledge.
Vedette	Italian/Old French	A sentinel.
Veena	Hindu	
Vega	Arabic	A falling star.
Velda		The chosen one.
Veleda	Teutonic	Inspired wisdom.
Velika	Slavonic	The great one.

Velma		A modern English name which is particularly popular in the USA.
Velvet	English	Soft as velvet.
Vendela	Scandinavian	
Venetia	Latin	A lady of Venice.
Ventura	Spanish	Good luck, happiness.
Venus	Latin	Beautiful. After the Roman goddess of beauty and love.
Vera	Latin/Russian	Latin: True. Russian: Faith.
Verbena	Latin	A sacred bough or plant.
Verda	Latin	Fresh.
Verena	Swiss	The name of a 3rd-century saint.
Verity	Latin/Old French	Truth.
Verla		Latin: True. Russian: Faith.
Verna	Latin	Springlike, fresh. The feminine form of Vernon. Also see Laverne.
Verona	Latin	After the Italian city. Also a variation of Veronica.
Veronica	Latin	A true likeness or image.
Verran	Cornish	The short one.
Verrin	Old French	
Verushka	Czech	Latin: True. Russian: Faith. A common name in Russia.
Vesna	Slavonic	Spring.
Vesper	Latin	Evening.
Vespera	Latin	An evening star.
Vesta	Latin	A guardian of the sacred fire. After the Roman goddess of the hearth.
Vevay	Welsh	White wave.
Vevette		A woman of the people.
Vevila	Irish Gaelic	The melodious one.
Vevina		Sweet lady.
Vibhuti	Hindu	
Vicki		Victory, the victorious one.
Vicky		Victory, the victorious one.
Victoria	Latin	Victory, the victorious one.
Vida	Hebrew	The beloved one. Short form of Davida, the feminine version of David.
Vidonia	Portuguese	A vine branch.

Vidya	Sanskrit	Knowledge.
Vienna	Latin	From wine country.
Viera	Latin/Russian	Latin: True. Russian: Faith.
Vigilia	Latin	Alert, vigilant.
Vikki		Victory, the victorious one.
Vikriti	Hindu	
Vilhelmina		The resolute protector. A feminine form of William.
Vilma		A modern English name which is particularly popular in the USA.
Vimala	Sanskrit	Pure.
Vina	Spanish	From the vineyard.
Vinata	Hindu	Humble, mother of Garuda.
Vinaya	Hindu	Good behavior.
Vincentia	Latin	The conqueror. The feminine form of Vincent.
Vinita	Hindu	
Vinvella	French	
Viola		A name made famous by the Shakespearian play Twelfth Night.
Violenta		From Shakespeare's play All's Well that Ends Well.
Violet	Latin	From the name of the flower.
Virgilia	Latin	A staff bearer.
Virginia	Latin	Maidenly, pure.
Virida	Latin	Green.
Viridis	Latin	youthful and blooming
Virini	Hindu	
Visala	Hindu	Celestial Apsara.
Vita	Latin	Life.
Vitoria	Spanish	Victory, the victorious one.
Vittoria	Italian	Victory, the victorious one.
Viveka	Scandinavian	Lively.
Vivian	Latin	Gracious in life or lively.
Viviana	Italian	Lovely.
Vivien	Latin	Full of life, vital.
Vivienne		Life.
Volante	Latin	The flying one.
Voleta	Greek	Veiled one.
Voletta	Greek/Old French	Veiled.

Volumnia		From Shakespeare's play Coriolanus.
Vonni		From the name Veronica and Yvonne. Veronica - A true likeness or image. Yvonne - French: An archer. Greek: The wood of the Yew tree.
Vonnie		From the name Veronica and Yvonne.
Vonny		From the name Veronica and Yvonne.
Vrinda	Hindu	Virtue and strength.
Vyvyan	Cornish	From an old surname.
Wahiba	Arabic	The generous one.
Wahida	Arabic	Unique.
Wakanda	Sioux	inner magical power
Walburga	Anglo-Saxon	a might defender, a fortress
Walda	German	A ruler.
Walida	Arabic	The newborn girl.
Wallis	Old French	A foreigner, particularly a woman from Wales.
Waltraud	Teutonic	Rule strength.
Wanda	Aboriginal/Teutonic	Aboriginal: A sandhill. Teutonic: A Slavonic woman, or a wanderer.
Waneta	Native American	Charger.
Wanetta	Old English	Pale.
Wanika	Hawaiian	God's gracious gift.
Wapeka	Native American	Skillful.
Waratah	Aboriginal	A red flower.
Warrah	Aboriginal	Honeysuckle.
Warrina	Aboriginal	To give.
Waseme	African	
Wasima	Arabic	Graceful, pretty.
Wateka		
Weema	Aboriginal	Small.
Wendi		From the name Wendy. Invented by J M Barrie in the early 1900s for his play Peter Pan.
Wendy	English	A name invented by J M Barrie in the early 1900s for his play Peter Pan.
Wenona	Native American	The firstborn daughter.
Wenonah	Native American	The firstborn daughter.

Whitney	Old English	From the white island.
Whoopi		
Widjan	Arabic	Ecstacy.
Wihtburth	Anglo-Saxon	
Wilda	Teutonic	The untamed one.
Wilfreda	Teutonic	Desiring peace. Feminine form of Wilfred.
Wilga	Aboriginal	A small tree.
Wilhelmina	Teutonic	The resolute protector. A feminine form of William.
Willa	Aboriginal	A woman or wife.
Willow	Old English	From the name of the Willow tree.
Wilma		The resolute protector.
Wilona	Old English	Desired.
Win		A prosperous friend. The feminine form of Edwin.
Winda	Swahili	Hunt.
Winema	Native American	A female chief.
Winifred	Teutonic/Welsh	Teutonic: A peaceful friend. Welsh: Joyful peace.
Winnie		A prosperous friend. The feminine form of Edwin.
Winona	Native American	The firstborn daughter.
Winsome	English	Pleasant and attractive.
Winter	Old English	Born in the winter months.
Wren	Old English	A tiny bird.
Wyanet	Native American	Beautiful.
Wylie	Old English	Wily or beguiling.
Wynfled	Anglo-Saxon	
Wynne	Cornish/Welsh	Fair, or blessed. Also a diminutive of Winifred.
Wynona	Native American	The firstborn daughter.
Wyuna	Aboriginal	Clear.
Xandy	Greek	Protector of man.
Xanthe	Greek	Yellow, bright or golden-haired.
Xaquelina	Galician	
Xaviera	Arabic/Spanish	Arabic: Brilliant, bright. Spanish: Of the new house. Feminine form of Xavier.
Xenia	Greek	Hospitable, welcoming.
Xenobia	Greek	

Ximena	Greek/Hebrew	Greek: A heroine. Hebrew: He heard.
Xiomara	Spanish	
Xuxa	Spanish	A Queen or ruler. Feminine form of Xerxes.
Xylia	Spanish	A Queen or ruler. Feminine form of Xerxes.
Xylia	Greek	Wood dweller.
Xylona	Greek	From the forest.
Xyza	Gothic	By the sea.
Yachi	Japanese	Eight thousand.
Yachne	Hebrew	Gracious.
Yael	Hebrew	A wild goat.
Yaffa	Hebrew	Beautiful.
Yaffah	Hebrew	Beautiful.
Yaksha	Hindu	A sister of Daksha.
Yamini	Hindu	
Yamuna	Hindi	A sacred river.
Yamura	Hindu	
Yangchen	Tibetan/Sherpa	The sacred one.
Yani	Aboriginal	Peace.
Yanira	Hebrew	
Yara	Aboriginal	A seagull.
Yaralla	Aboriginal	A camp.
Yaravi	Yari, Yara	
Yarmilla	Slavic	Merchant.
Yarrah	Aboriginal	A river red gum.
Yasmeen	Persian	A fragrant flower.
Yasmin	Persian	A fragrant flower.
Yasmina	Persian	A fragrant flower.
Yasmine	Persian	A fragrant flower.
Yasu	Japanese	Tranquil.
Yavonna	Hebrew	
Yayoi	Japanese	March.
Ydel	Hebrew	Praise.
Yedda	Old English	A singer, one with a melodious voice.
Yehudi	Hebrew	Praise to the Lord, a person from Judah.
Yehudit	Jewish	A modern form of Judith.
Yejide	Yoruba	Image of her mother.

Yelena	Russian	The light of the sun.
Yeliz	Turkish	
Yemena	Hebrew	
Yenene	Miwok Indian	Wizard poisoning a sleeping person.
Yesmina	Hebrew	Right hand, strength.
Yetta	Old English/German	To give. Also a diminutive of the name Henrietta.
Yeva	Russian	Live-giving.
Yevon	Hebrew	
Yindi	Aboriginal	The sun.
Ylwa	Scandinavian	She-wolf.
Ynes	Spanish	Pure, chaste. Forms of the girl's name Agnes.
Ynez	Spanish	Pure, chaste.
Yogini	Hindu	
Yogita	Hindu	
Yoko	Japanese	Positive.
Yolanda	Greek/Old French	A violet flower.
Yomaris	Spanish	I am the sun.
Yon	Korean	A lotus blossom.
Yona	Hebrew/Native American	Hebrew: A dove. Native American: A bear.
Yoninah	Hebrew	Dove.
Yooralla	Aboriginal	Love.
Yootha		Thirsty.
Yori	Japanese	Trustworthy.
Yoshi	Japanese	Good.
Yoshiko	Japanese	Child of Yoshi.
Yovela	Hebrew	Rejoicing.
Yrsa	Scandinavian	
Ysabel		A form of Elizabeth, meaning consecrated to God.
Yseult		The fair one.
Ysobel	Spanish	A form of Elizabeth, meaning consecrated to God.
Ysolda		The fair one.
Ysolde		The fair one.
Ytha		Thirsty.
Yukako	Japanese	Child of Yuka.
Yukiko	Japanese	Child of Yuki.
Yumako	Japanese	Child of Yuma.

Yumi	Japanese	Beauty.
Yumiko	Japanese	Child of Yumi
Yungara	Aboriginal	A wife.
Yuri	Aboriginal/Russian	Aboriginal: To hear. Also the Russian form of George.
Yuriko	Japanese	Child of Yuri.
Yusra	Arabic	The prosperous one.
Yutsuko	Japanese	Child of Yutso.
Yvette	French	From the name Yvonne. The feminine form of Yves. The little archer.
Yvonne	French/Greek	French: An archer. Greek: The wood of the Yew tree.
Zabrina		A legendary character.
Zada	Arabic	The lucky one.
Zagir	Armenian	A flower.
Zagros	sweet, feminine	
Zahara	Arabic/Hebrew	Arabic: A blossom or flower. Hebrew: The bright dawn.
Zahava	Hebrew	Golden.
Zahra	Arabic/Hebrew	Arabic: A blossom or flower. Hebrew: The bright dawn.
Zaida	Arabic	Fortunate one.
Zaira	Arabic	Rose.
Zakia	Hebrew	Bright, pure.
Zalia	Hebrew	
Zalika	Arabic/Swahili	Well-born.
Zaltana	Native American	High mountain.
Zama	Latin	Came from Zama.
Zambda	Hebrew	Meditation.
Zan	Hebrew	
Zana		
Zandra		The defender, or helper of mankind.
Zane	Hebrew	God is gracious.
Zaneta	Hebrew	The grace of God.
Zanita	Greek	Long teeth.
Zankhana	Hindu	
Zanna	English	A lily.
Zara	Arabic/Hebrew	Arabic: A blossom or flower. Hebrew: The bright dawn.

Zaria		Helped by God.
Zarifa	Arabic	Graceful.
Zarna	Hindu	
Zavanna		From the grasslands or open plains.
Zayit	Hebrew	
Zaylin	Zayla, Aylin	
Zaza	Hebrew, Arabic	Movement, flowery.
Zdenka	Czech	One from Sidon, a winding sheet.
Zea	Latin	Ripened grain.
Zeanes	Hebrew	
Zebina	Greek	One who is gifted.
Zee	Hebrew	
Zeeba		
Zehava	Hebrew	Golden.
Zeitia	Galician	
Zelah	Hebrew	A side. Also a Cornish location.
Zelda		The grey battle heroine. From the name Griselda. Made famous by the wife of American writer F. Scott Fitzgerald.
Zelena	Greek	The goddess of the moon.
Zelenka	Czech	little innocent one
Zelia	Greek	Zealous, devoted to one's duty.
Zelinda	Old German	Shield of victory.
Zelma		A divine helmet.
Zelpha	Hebrew	
Zena	Scottish	The defender, or helper of mankind.
Zenaide	Greek	One who has devoted his life to God.
Zenda	Persian	A sacred woman.
Zenia	Greek	Hospitable.
Zenith	Arabic	The highest point.
Zennor	Cornish	The name of a village.
Zenobia	Greek	Given life by Zeus.
Zephyrine	Greek	A breeze, the west wind.
Zera	Greek	Seeds.
Zerlina	Teutonic	Serene beauty.
Zerlinda	Hebrew	Beautiful dawn.
Zeruah	Hebrew	

Zethel	Hebrew	
Zeva	Greek	A sword.
Zevida	Hebrew	Gift.
Zhalore	Hebrew	
Zia	Arabic	Splendor or ripened grain.
Ziahon	Hebrew	
Ziazan	Armenian	Rainbow.
Zigana	Hungarian	Gypsy girl.
Zila	Hebrew	Shadow.
Zilia	Aragonese	
Zillah	Hebrew	Shade or a shadow. A biblical name.
Zilli		My shadow.
Zina	African	
Zinaida	Greek	Of Zeus.
Zinnia	Latin	From the flower.
Ziona	Hebrew	A sign.
Zippora	Hebrew	A little bird, a sparrow. A biblical name.
Zisel	Hebrew	Sweet.
Zita	Italian	The name of a 13th-century Tuscan saint. Also a diminutive of Rosita (See Rosa).
Ziva	Hebrew	Brightness.
Zizi	Hungarian	dedicated to God
Zoe	Greek	Life.
Zoey	Greek	Life.
Zofeya	Hebrew	God sees.
Zofia	Polish	Wisdom.
Zohra	Arabic	Blooming.
Zoila	child	
Zola		Life.
Zoleen	Hebrew	
Zona	Latin	Prostitute.
Zonda	Hebrew	
Zora	Slavonic	Dawn.
Zosia	Polish	Wisdom.
Zosima	Greek	Lively.
Zotia	Polish	One with wisdom
Zsa-Zsa	Hungarian	A Lily. From the name Susan.
Zula	Hebrew	

Zuleika	Persian	Brilliant beauty.
Zulema	Arabic/Hebrew	Peace.
Zuri	Swahili	Beautiful.
Zuriaa	Basque	
Zuza	Czech	Graceful lily.
Zuzana	Czech	A lily.
Zuzanna	Polish	A lily.

Made in the USA
San Bernardino, CA
16 December 2012